OPINION WRITING AND DRAFTING IN CONTRACT LAW

Carron-Ann Russell, LLM
of the Middle Temple, Barrister,
Attorney-at-Law, Jamaica,
Senior Lecturer,
Inns of Court School of Law

Cavendish
Publishing
Limited

First published in Great Britain 1996 by Cavendish Publishing Limited,
The Glass House, Wharton Street London WC1X 9PX

Telephone: 0171-278 8000
Facsimile: 0171-278 8080

British Library Cataloguing in Publication Data. A catalogue record for this book is available from the British Library.

Russell, Carron-Ann
Opinion Writing and Drafting in Contract Law
I Title
808.0663441062

ISBN 1-85941-030 8

Printed and bound in Great Britain

Preface

The aim of this book is to provide an integrated guide of opinion writing and drafting in the law of contract. It will be of use to the Vocational Bar student, intending and non-intending practitioners, Law Society students and students studying for law degrees.

I am grateful to the staff at Cavendish Publishing for giving me the opportunity to participate in this series and especially to Kate Nicol for her patient and sensitive approach. To Hogath Andall, for his help in research and typing at such short notice. To all my old Bar students wherever you are in the Commonwealth. Any errors or omissions are my own and in no way reflect on the publisher. Suggestions and discussions on the case papers are warmly invited.

To Jah – one love.

CAR
December 1995

C

**University of
Hertfordshire**

Law Learning Resources Centre

Law Division, Hatfield Road, St Albans AL1 3RS
Tel 01707 284235 internal X 3235

This book is in heavy demand and is due back strictly by
the last date stamped below. A fine will be charged for
overdue items.

ONE WEEK LOAN

Cavendish
Publishing
Limited

Contents

Table of Cases

Table of Statutes

Introduction

This book is not intended to prescribe a certain way to write an opinion or to draft pleadings. There is no prescribed way to do either, subject to any directions from the White Book in respect of pleadings, but there are accepted formats. This book attempts to act as a guide, not a precedent, to analysing, preparing and writing an opinion and drafting certain basic pleadings.

Both opinion writing and drafting skills are fundamental tools which need to be developed in order to become a competent practitioner. These skills are not easily taught but rather are learned. The most this book can do, therefore, is to provide ideas on how students can teach themselves, with professional guidance, the accepted way to do both tasks.

It may appear that some of the ideas suggested seem facile and self-evident. However, in my experience the transfer from a student-focused, academic approach to law, to a practical professional methodology, is a quantum leap and not automatic. Therefore some steps to use as a guide may prove useful in achieving this transfer. However, ultimately, whichever approach students choose to adopt is personal and will be reflected in the conduct of their legal work.

This book simply seeks to suggest ideas which have been tried, tested and proven successful. I hope the reader will find it of some value at the early stages of their legal training.

CAR
August 1995

1   Opinion writing and drafting

Some guidelines

The lawyer's main goal when retained by instructing solicitors should invariably be to help their client by giving sound, fair, impartial and professional advice. The lawyer, after thorough research, should know the relevant area of law on which he is to advise.

The purpose of counsel's opinion is, as the title suggests, to give a view or opinion or to advise the clients of what their chances are in relation to their case, and whether the matter is worth pursuing from a litigation/negotiation point of view. The opinion is written by counsel and is seen initially by a solicitor who then has a conference with the client to inform them of counsel's advice or view about the matter at hand. The style and format of the opinion, therefore, should be practically oriented and written in a way that allows the solicitor to translate counsel's view clearly and easily to the client, without confusing them with complex issues of law. What the client wants to know from his legal advisers is what his chances are of succeeding in his action or defending it.

In this regard, then, counsel's opinion need not be overly legalistic in its approach. The solicitor will know the law. What he wants to know from counsel is his expert opinion on practical matters: for example, whether damages are likely to be awarded in this particular case, and if so how much, or what the next practical or tactical step to take should be, or what the merits of the case are. The lawyer's opinion should therefore be a legal framework on which counsel builds the opinion. Counsel should be analysing the facts and relating those facts to the law, not to abstract principles of law. Counsel is also writing the opinion as a reminder to himself for future purposes, should the matter not proceed immediately to trial but come to trial at a later date. If the opinion is clear and succinct, counsel will be able to resurrect the legal issues quickly without having to trawl through all the case papers again. It is tempting to read the brief and assume that all the facts are absorbed. Often small details can be overlooked, or, if the matter is quite complex, then the significance of certain issues will be more difficult to grasp.

The opinion serves another purpose: it is useful to jog counsel's mind when, at some later occasion, he comes to look at the papers on which he will need to take action in relation to the case. A well-written opinion depends on a clear and accurate analysis of the facts scenario found in documents and statements of both lay and expert witnesses and an interpretation of instructions given by those instructing counsel. The key to careful analysis is a sound method for managing, understanding and organising the facts of the case, identifying the legal and factual issues and dealing with each issue step by step, chronological-ly and examining any possible legal implications that may arise in the sequence of events.

Very often the initial opinion written by counsel would be his preliminary view of the case. He will put his views as best he can, based on the information he has been sent by instructing solicitors. It is often the case, however, that counsel will have to request further information before being able to write a final opinion.

The red pencil test: a DIY guide

(1)   An initial reading of the papers with an open mind as to what view will be taken.

(2)   A clear understanding of what instructing solicitors have asked counsel to do in relation to the case.

(3)   A second reading of the papers with a red pencil underlining issues and concepts that seem to be pertinent to what has been instructed.

(4)   A third reading isolating under the headings the following in note form:

- *Dramatis personae*, ie plaintiff, defendant, lay witnesses, expert witnesses;
- Dates and times;
- Places;
- Relevant figures;
- Factual issues;
- Legal issues;
- Case for and/or against both plaintiff and defendant;
- Evidential difficulties;
- Procedural difficulties;
- Missing information, such as plans, photographs, maps, reports;
- Strength of the case for and against both plaintiff and defendant;
- Proposed action.

Dramatis personae

Under this heading all parties must be identified. At this stage is not important to determine whether the particular person is a relevant party to the action. It may be that this person, although not a major player, ie plaintiff or defendant, is and could be a relevant party at a later stage, ie a third party to whom some lia-bility may be attached or, indeed, a useful witness.

Dates and times

All dates and times should be highlighted and noted in chronological order. This will help to set the story in its sequential order and to identify any missing event or lapse of time. It will also confirm that the action is within the limitation period prescribed by statute if litigation is being considered.

Places

The *locus in quo* might be a significant or disputed issue in the matter. Dates and places should be correlated.

Relevant figures

Quantum, costs and liability are three of the most important issues around which many actions revolve. It is important therefore to identify the basis on which any award may be made or the likely cost that any proposed party to the action may face by looking at the relevant figures in the case. Tabulated heads are useful for identifying figures, in an effort to assess what the overall final amounts could be.

Factual issues

Identifying the factual issues clearly is obviously one of the most important tasks to be undertaken in order to produce a sound opinion. A thorough analysis of the facts needs to be made in order to get a total overview of the client's position in relation to the law. A factual analysis will also help counsel to determine where the gaps and inconsistencies lie in his case, what the cause of action is likely to be and what, if any, are the potential remedies.

Legal issues

Counsel will need to know what the relevant legal issues are. Not only the major and patent issues but very often ancillary issues: whether a particular person can be joined in the action, whether the limitation period has expired and what the consequences are likely to be. The legal issues should be firmly related to the facts of the particular case. The opinion is not a legal treatise but a combination of the law as a broadsheet on which to place and interrelate the facts.

Case for and against both plaintiff and defendant

Counsel will be instructed on behalf of either the plaintiff or the defendant, and the focus of his advice will be on that party. However, in advising his client, counsel will need to be aware of the other side's case and must be willing to take account of any adverse evidence likely to affect the outcome. He should advise accordingly, anticipating what the other party is likely to raise.

Evidential difficulties

These matters can determine the success or failure of the case. Counsel should anticipate what further evidence will be needed and must request it from instructing solicitors. Counsel should expect that the strength of his case will depend largely on the possibility of adducing the relevant evidence to support his case and rebut the opponent's version of events.

Procedural difficulties

Counsel should ascertain from the papers whether any time limits are imminent, whether they will cause difficulty and should deal with them appropriately. Instructing solicitors will often rely on counsel to advise on the next procedural step.

Missing information

Information in the form of documentary evidence, plans, reports, maps, photographs, real evidence may not be among the papers sent to counsel by instructing solicitors. If these exist, they could throw new light on the eventual success or otherwise of the case. Counsel should request missing information from instructing solicitors in specific form, for example, a further statement from the plaintiff clarifying X, or an expert report from Y. On receipt of this information, counsel will need to amend or confirm the view expressed in his opinion, and advises how the missing information could enhance or detract from the success of his client's case.

Strength of the case

More than anything else the client will want to know how robust or weak his position is in relation to his opponent's case. From the papers, counsel should be able to predict a realistic outcome without building up false hopes. Counsel should be objective and truthful about the prospects of the case; this should be communicated clearly and concisely in the opinion.

Proposed action

Instructing solicitors may want to know what the next step should be based on counsel's opinion: should proceedings be issued forthwith, should a defence be filed, should negotiations take place or should a conference be called? In the opinion counsel will be expected to anticipate what the next course of action should be and advise instructing solicitors. Having organised all the information in a manageable form and grasped the thrust of the main issues, the next step is to write the opinion.

Format of the opinion

The opinion should start with a general brief summary of the facts of the case and a restatement of what the instructing solicitor has instructed counsel to do. A paragraph summarising counsel's advice should then follow, stating clearly the conclusions counsel has reached and what should be done. The following paragraphs should be numbered, sequentially with sub-headed paragraphs, dealing with the various issues and considering the relevant factors as listed above. The final paragraph should draw all the threads of the opinion together, reaffirming counsel's view of the case.

Basic guidelines of drafting and pleadings

Instructing solicitors will sometimes know what pleadings he wants counsel to draft and will make a specific request for that pleading. At other times counsel will be asked to draft appropriate pleadings. The draft pleadings are to accompany the opinion and are equally if not more important than the opinion because it is destined not for the client but for the court and the judge's sight. From the pleadings the judge will be able to gather what the main issues of the case are and get an overview of the whole case scenario. Pleadings should be clear and concise. The formal parts of the pleadings are governed by rules of the Supreme Court/County Court and should be adhered to rigidly. The rest of the body of pleadings should tell the story of the case from the point of view of counsel who is drafting it. Pleadings should not be clustered with unnecessary information but should be incisive in isolating the client's case. In the pleadings counsel should state the facts and not his unsupported opinion or allegations made by the client.

RSC Order 18 r 6 gives specific details about the form of pleadings:

(a) Each pleading in an action must bear on its face:

    (i) the year in which the writ in the action was issued and the letter and number of the action;

    (ii) the title of the action;

    (iii) the division of the High Court to which the action is assigned and the name of the judge (if any) to whom it is assigned;

    (iv) a description of the pleading;

    (v) the date on which it was served

(b) Every pleading must if necessary be divided into paragraphs numbered consecutively, each allegation being so far as convenient contained in a separate paragraph.

(c) Dates, sums and other numbers must be expressed in a pleading in figures and not in words.

(d) Every pleading of a party must be endorsed:

    (i)   where the party sues or defends in person with his name and address;

    (ii)   in any other case with the name or firm and business address of a solicitor by whom it was served and also (if the solicitor is the agent of another) the name or firm and business address of his principal.

(e)   Every pleading of a party must be signed by counsel, is settled by him and if not by the party's solicitor or by the party if he sues or defends in person.

Order 18 r 7 clearly states that counsel should plead facts and not evidence:

(a)   Subject to the provision of this rule and rules 7a, 10, 11, 12 every pleading must contain and contain only a statement in summary form of the material facts on which the party pleading relies for his claim or defence as the case may be, but not the evidence by which those facts are to be proved and the statement must be as brief as the nature of the case permits.

(b)   Without prejudice to the previous paragraph the effect of any document or the purport of any conversation referred to in the pleading must as material be briefly stated and the precise words of the document for conversation shall not be stated except insofar as those words are themselves material.

(c)   A party need not plead any fact if it presumed by law to be true or the burden of disproving it lies on the other party unless the other party has specifically denied it in his pleading.

(d)   The statement that a thing has been done or that an event has occurred, being a thing or event the doing or occurrence of which as the case may be constitutes a condition precedent necessary for the case of a party is to be implied in his pleading. Order 18 rule 11 allows law to be pleaded in exceptional cases. A party may by his pleading raise any point of law.

Order 18 r 12 outlines what particulars should be pleaded:

(1)   Subject to paragraph 2 every pleading must contain the necessary particulars of any claim, defence or other matter pleaded including without prejudice to the generality of the foregoing words:

    (i)   particular of any misrepresentation, fraud, breach of trust, wilful default or undue influence on which the party pleading relies and

    (ii)   where a party pleading alleges any condition of the mind of any person, whether any disorder or disability of mind or any malice, fraudulent intention or other condition of mind, except knowledge, particulars of the facts on which the party relies.

(2)   Where it is necessary to give particulars of debt, expenses or damages and those particulars exceed three folios they must be set out in a separate document, referred to in the pleading and the pleading must state whether the document has already been served and if so when or is to be served with the pleading.

Various types of pleadings

Statement/particulars of claim

In this pleading the plaintiff will tell the story from his point of view, stating his case by setting out the allegations he is making against the other side, and particularising what injury or damage he has suffered as a result of the other side's actions.

The statement or particulars of claim will be the pleadings that will start the formal court action.

The defence

In response to the plaintiff's claim, the defendant, if he intends to defend the action, will respond by serving on the plaintiff his answer in the form of a defence. In this pleading, the defendant will either admit, deny or make no admissions about the various parts of the plaintiff's claim as presented in the statement/particulars of claim.

Third-party notice

This pleading seeks to join an additional party to the main action, obviating the need to institute fresh proceedings. A third-party notice is normally incurred by the defendant who alleges that a third party is partially or wholly to blame for the action which has been brought against him, and he therefore wants to join that party in the current action.

A third-party notice can stand effectively as the defendant's statement of claim against the third party he seeks to join.

Further and better particulars

If pleadings are ambiguous and unclear, the court has power by virtue of RSC Order 18 r 12(7) to order a party to serve Further and Better Particulars to clarify the ambiguity at the request of the other party. If served after a request, the document is regarded as a pleading, and must answer specific points requested by the other side.

Counterclaims

A counterclaim allows a defendant in any action who alleges that he has a claim or any relief against a plaintiff in the action to make a claim by serving a counterclaim appended to his defence in the same action.

Order 15 r 2(1) states:

A defendant in any action who alleges that he has any claim or is entitled to any relief or remedy against a plaintiff in the action in respect of any matter (whenever and however arising) may, instead of bringing a separate action, make a counterclaim in respect of that matter, and where he does so he must add the counterclaim to his defence.

2 Formation of the contract

The purpose of this chapter is not to give a comprehensive summary of the law relating to offer and acceptance, but to concentrate generally on a number of central issues which could form the basis of litigation and which will also help to illustrate the technique of analysis in fact management and opinion writing in this area.

This chapter looks at the essential ingredients that make up the basis on which the contract is formed and the process by which parties to a contract reach agreement. English law provides guidelines which help to determine which promises are legally enforceable. *Prima facie* it could be argued that all promises should be kept and the promisor should be bound by the promise they make. A promise by Malcolm to take Marlene out to a restaurant for a meal could be seen to be a completely different situation from one where Lyn promises to buy Frank's television set for £250.00. In the second situation, most people would argue that if Lyn fails to honour her promise, Frank should have some legal recourse, while in the first case it would seem inconceivable that Malcolm should be bound by his promise. Although there may seem to be a sound legal basis for enforcing that second promise, it seems that both parties agreed to the terms: Frank placed reliance on Lyn's promise and as a result suffered financial loss. In some instances, for example, promises made by family members, there is some doubt whether the promise would in certain cases have legal force.

For a contract to be legally enforceable, three crucial elements must be present:

- agreement between the parties (offer and acceptance);
- bargain (consideration); and
- contractual intention.

Offer and acceptance

Parties usually reach an agreement by the making of an offer and an acceptance of that offer. The offer and the acceptance need not be in writing and can be made by way of a promise. In situations where the agreement leaves acts to be performed by both parties, the contract is described as a bilateral contract; if those acts are outstanding to be performed by only one side, then the contract is regarded as a unilateral contract. An offer is a statement made by the offeror, the person making the statement who accepts to contract on terms stated and agrees to be bound by the statement when it is accepted by the offeree, the person accepting to be bound by the offer on those terms. An offer may be made expressly or by conduct; it may be made to one person, to a group or to the world at large.

An important aspect of an offer is that the offeror must intend to be bound by the offeree, accepting those terms of the agreement without further negotiation. Great care must therefore be taken to distinguish between an offer which is legally binding and an invitation to treat where the offeror invites the offeree to make an offer, and has no legal status. An invitation to treat is perhaps best explained by examples: statements of prices, goods on display at a price in shop windows, or on supermarket's shelves, catalogues and circulars offering goods for sale, an advertisement for an upcoming auction, enquiries about wages, and job qualifications for a particular job. In the classic case of *Fisher v Bell* (1960) a shopkeeper had displayed a knife in a shop window with a price tag on it and described it as an ejector knife. The shopkeeper was prosecuted for offering for sale a flick knife contrary to s 1(1) of the Offensive Weapons Act 1959. The court held that the shopkeeper was not guilty of the offence because the displaying of the knife in the shop was an invitation to treat and was therefore not a contravention of the statute.

Invitation to treat

Not all displays and advertisements are to be regarded as invitations to treat. In *Carlill v Carbolic Smoke Ball Co* (1892), the court held in the plaintiff's favour in deciding on a number of issues raised in the pleadings, that it is possible to make an offer to the whole world. In a more recent case, *Thornton v Shoe Lane Parking Ltd* (1971), it is said that a notice which was displayed at the entrance of a car-park was an offer not an invitation to treat, because the only act of acceptance necessary was driving into the car-park.

In situations where there is dispute about whether the parties were in agreement at the material time, the courts apply an objective test to ascertain what the parties meant. Inferences are drawn from the circumstances of the negotiations as to what the parties intended, and their words and conduct are analysed with a view to determining whether they intended to contract on certain terms, whether the offer was made, communicated and accepted. Any acceptance made by the offeree must relate to the terms of the offer; if the offeree makes a counter offer it negates the original offer so that it cannot be accepted subsequently, and it is also tantamount to a rejection of the offer. In *Hyde v Wrench* (1849), D offered to sell P a farm for £1,000. P made an offer of £950 which D refused. P then at a later date said he would pay the £1,000 and sued to enforce the contract. The court held that no contract existed. By making a counter offer of £950, P had rejected and nullified D's original offer and it was not possible for him to revive the original offer by a later acceptance.

It is generally the rule that the offeree must comply with the terms of the offer requiring communication of the acceptance to the offeror. Any doubt as to whether the acceptance has been communicated effectively must rest with the offeree.

There are exceptions to the general rule relating to acceptance: these refer to communications by post or telegram/telemessages. The rule holds as a matter of convenience to the offeree that the acceptance takes place as soon as the letter is posted. A number of restrictions are placed on the rule that help give it a common sense perspective: the letter must be properly stamped and addressed, it must be reasonable to use the post in all the circumstances of the case.

The factual analysis: opinion writing

The main aspects and issues of important areas have now been analysed giving a basis upon which a case problem relating to those issues can be examined, and the tools for opinion writing exhibited. The rest of this chapter will concentrate on demonstrating the opinion writing/fact management technique, with accompanying pleadings.

CASE SCENARIO

Counsel is instructed by Dobb & Co Solicitors. Counsel has herewith statement of Mr Ian Kinco. Counsel is asked to advise what Mr Kinco's position is in relation to the following facts. Counsel will see that instructing solicitors have summarised the situation as best as possible, as no statements are yet to hand and no supporting documents are yet ready. These will be forwarded to counsel as soon as they are prepared.

Summary of statement

Mr Joshua Smuck placed an advert in the *Wisebourne Times*, published 3 June, in the following terms: A brilliant buy – 20 new mobile phones at £75 each. Will go to the first 20 replies received enclosing a cheque for £75. Send a cheque to 10 The Green, Carshalton, Sutton.

On 9 June, Mr Kinco posted his letter to the above address sending £75 cash and confirming that he wished to buy a mobile phone. Unfortunately it seems that Monotone, the company on which Mr Smuck was relying for his stocks, had become insolvent. Mr Smuck placed an apology in the· *Wisebourne Times* on 10 June announcing that the phones were no longer available

It would appear that Mr Kinco's letter arrived on 11 June and was one of the first 20 to be received. Would counsel please advise accordingly and settle appropriate pleadings.

The practical approach

The primary task that needs to be done is a clear analysis of the facts presented, looking closely at chronology, dates and *dramatis personae*. The facts should be taken step by step, examining any possible implications that may arise at each stage. The issues to be resolved therefore must be:

Legal/factual issues

- The state of the advertisement: is it an invitation to treat or an offer?
- How will the court assess the parties' intention?
- Was Mr Smuck willing to be bound by an acceptance without more?
- Does Mr Kinco accept Mr Smuck's offer by sending his letter on 9 June?
- Has Mr Kinco satisfied all the conditions of the purported offer?
- What is the significance of Mr Smuck's withdrawal of the offer on 10 June?

- Is it effective as published?
- What is the nature of the contract?
- Has Mr Kinco suffered any detriment by the apparent breach?
- What is the strength of the evidence in Mr Kinco's favour?
- Should proceedings be issued and to what avail?

Dramatis personae

- Mr Kinco – putative plaintiff, alleging breach of contract;
- Mr Smuck – putative defendant;
- Monotone Ltd, suppliers – should they be joined as putative defendant third-party by Mr Kinco?

Gaps in instructions: to be requested

- Evidence of the date of the arrival of the letter;
- Copy of the letter;
- Evidence of posting;
- Copy of Mr Smuck's advertisement.

THE OPINION

Ian Kinco v Joshua Smuck

1   I am instructed by Dobb & Co Solicitors on behalf of Mr Kinco who feels aggrieved by what he sees as a breach of contract by Mr Smuck in failing to deliver the mobile phone ordered by post. I am grateful to instructing solicitors for a summary of the factual details and in spite of the missing documents will endeavour to advise as instructed.

2   **Advertisement: offer or invitation to treat**

The first issue to be resolved is whether the advertisement contained an offer or an invitation to treat. In deciding the question the court will look at the intention of Mr Smuck, the offeror; this will be assessed objectively. The court will have regard to the circumstances of the offer and any other expressed or implicit indicators that would support the advertisement as an offer. It is my opinion that the court will look at the wording of the offer, especially 'will go to', and may be willing to impute to Mr Smuck an intention to be bound, thereby satisfying one of the fundamental ingredients of an offer.

3   **Unilateral contract**

Mr Smuck has unilaterally made a promise to sell mobile phones to whichever reader of the advertisement fulfils the requisite conditions, that is by sending a cheque for £75 and replying by a fixed date. Mr Kinco made no promises himself and also it could be argued, and I envisage that perhaps this is what Mr Smuck will say, is that the advert was an invitation to treat and not an offer. It is my view that the court relying on such cases as *Carlill v Carbolic Smoke Ball Co* (1893), will apply an objective test in order to find that an offer was in fact made. Does Mr Kinco's letter of 11 June constitute a valid acceptance of the offer? A potential difficulty which may seem to arise is whether by sending cash when a cheque was stipulated Mr Kinco has fulfilled the conditions required by Mr Smuck. The question is: was that stipulated requirement a mandatory one and by failing to satisfy that requirement has Mr Smuck not complied with the required terms? Although I have not seen a copy of the advertisement, from what instructing solicitors tell me, there is nothing to suggest a prohibition on any other form of payment as long as the total received amounted to £75. Naturally on receiving the advertisement my opinion may vary if there is anything to indicate that the cheque requirement was a mandatory requirement of the contract. Provisionally it is my opinion that on the facts before me there was valid acceptance.

4   Finally, the question still left to be answered is whether Mr Smuck's offer is still open after the arrival of Mr Kinco's letter. Mr Smuck purports to withdraw his offer on 10 June. I am not told however whether Mr Smuck's withdrawal has been communicated to Mr Kinco, which is the usual requirement. However, instructing solicitors inform me that Mr Smuck has published an apology in the *Wisebourne Times.* I am not told when Mr Kinco became aware of this advertisement. Could those instructing me kindly send me details of this, and whether this ad appeared in the next issue of the *Wisebourne Times.* It does seem to me in any event, and certainly an argument open to Mr Smuck that the notice revoking as soon as he had received acceptance is reasonable. This is a fairly strong argument in Mr Smuck's favour and does in my view lead me to believe that Mr Kinco does not have a good chance of recovering any damages in the circumstances, since Mr Kinco, as far as I am aware has not suffered any detriment by this purported reliance. I am at this stage speculating that this is the case, but should the opposite position be the real situation, could those instructing me kindly update me with these details in relation to reliance.

5   An evidential point which may prove a difficulty for Mr Kinco is proof of receipt of the letter to Mr Smuck within the time stipulated. If the letter had not been received as per the terms of the contract, this would significantly weaken Mr Kinco's already weak position. It is my opinion that subject to receiving further information from instructing solicitors, Mr Kinco does not have a strong case and should seriously consider the cost implications of pursuing this matter. Instructing solicitors will see that I have not addressed the question of whether Mr Smuck should join Monotone Ltd as third party. It is my opinion that this should not be our concern at this stage, as this is a course of events open to Mr Smuck. Instructing solicitors will find attached herewith a draft copy of statement of claim; instructing solicitors will see that I have left the details of particulars of loss blank, as I still await this information.

B A Barrister
7 Kings Court
Chancery Lane
London W11

15

The Wisebourne County Court   Case no

Between

Ian Kinco: *Plaintiff*

and

Joshua Smuck: *Defendant*

STATEMENT OF CLAIM

---

1   The plaintiff is and was at all material times an agent of a retail outlet, 'The Zones'. The defendant was the vendor of mobile telephones.

2   By a contract contained in an advertisement printed in the *Wisebourne Times* dated 3 June 1994 the plaintiff agreed to purchase and the defendant agreed to sell, a Spynx 90 mobile telephone for the sum of £75.00.

3   It was an express term of the contract that to be eligible to purchase the said telephone, the purchase price should arrive at 10 The Green, Carshalton, Sutton, among the first 20 replies, after the appearance of the advertisement.

4   It was an implied term of the contract that the said telephones would be available for sale.

5   By an advertisement dated 10 June 1994, the defendant wrongly, and in breach of the agreement, refuted the contract. The plaintiff, as he was entitled to do, accepted the said revocation.

6   By reason of the matters aforesaid, the plaintiff has suffered loss and damage.

Particulars

(a)   Loss of business: £

(b)   Loss of profit: £

7   Further the plaintiff claims interest pursuant to section 69 of the County Courts Act 1984 on the amount found to be due to the plaintiff at such rate and for such period as the court thinks fit.

AND the plaintiff claims:

(i)   Damages

(ii) The aforesaid interest pursuant to section 69 of the County Courts Act 1984 to be assessed.

B A Barrister
7 Kings Walk
Chancery Lane
WC1

3   Consideration

Introduction

It is a general principle of English law that a promise is not as a rule enforceable in the courts unless it is formalised by incorporation as a deed under seal or supported by 'consideration'. The purpose of the requirement of consideration is to put some legal limits on the enforceability of agreement when it is informal and gratuitous. The most well known of the numerous definitions of valuable consideration is that of Lush J in *Currie v Misa* (1875) that consideration is 'some right, interest, profit or benefit accruing to the one party or some forbearance, detriment loss or responsibility, given, suffered or undertaken by the other'.

The central feature of the doctrine is the idea of reciprocity: 'something of value in the eye of the law' must be given for a promise in order to make it enforceable as a contract. An informal or gratuitous promise does not amount to a contract. The traditional definition concentrates on the requirement that 'something of value' must be given in return for a promise. However, this is reinterpreted to mean that consideration is either some detriment to the promisee or some benefit to the promisor. While it is usual for the promisee to suffer detriment and create a benefit for the promisor, the promisee may provide consideration by doing anything that he was not legally bound to do, whether or not it actually occasions a detriment to him or confers a benefit on the promisor.

It is also well settled that mutual promises can be consideration for each other. Hence, for example, if Yvonne promises to deliver goods to Henry in six months time and for Henry to pay for them on delivery, there is an immediate binding contract from which neither party can withdraw, though performance cannot be claimed until the appointed time. However, a mere mutual desire behind a promise does not form legal consideration. This is so even if the promisor and the promisee share a mutual motive. If May promises to give Alex £500 to buy some new clothes, and hearing this Ayron goes out and spends £500 on a designer jacket only to find that Naomi later reneges on her promise and refuses to give him the money, Alex will find that he does not have an enforceable claim against May. Despite May's promise and the motive behind it, Alex cannot sue her for the money. Alex offered nothing of value in the eye of the law to May in exchange for the promise; in short there was no consideration for the promise. Similarly in the case of *Thomas v Thomas* (1842), a husband's desire that his widow should live in his house after his death was held not to be part of the consideration for the executor's promise that she could do so.

Adequacy of consideration

Under the doctrine of consideration a promise has no contractual force unless some value has been given for it. However, the courts do not in general ask whether adequate value has been given, or whether the agreement is one-sided or in other words 'a bad bargain'. The reason for this is simple. The fact that a contract is a bad deal for one party or a particularly good deal for the other does not affect the essential legal validity of the contract. The mere fact that a contracting party pays 'too much' or 'too little' for something is not irrelevant as it may provide cogent and compelling evidence of a fraud, a mistake, a breach of warranty, frustration or even the abuse of a fiduciary relationship.

Past consideration

The consideration for a promise must be given in return for the promise. If Susan makes a present of her old motor car to Celia and a year later Celia promises to pay Susan £750 there is no consideration for Celia's promise as Susan did not give Celia the car in return for it. In this case the old car is not good consideration; it is instead 'past consideration' and therefore bad. In determining whether consideration is past, the court will look to see if the consideration and the promise are substantially one transaction. The order of the events is not decisive. However, what is significant is the interval between consideration and promise. The longer the interval, the more likely the classification as past consideration is to be made. Whether in a particular case consideration is past or not is a question of fact. In *Re McArdle* (1951), a woman carried out work to a house jointly owned by members of her family. After the work had been completed, her relatives signed a document promising to pay her for the work. it was held that she could not recover the sum promised, as her consideration was past.

The test of whether an act done before a promise was made can be consideration is threefold: the act must have been done at the request of the promisor; it must have been understood that payment would be made; and the payment if it had been promised in advance must be legally recoverable. Therefore, if Celia had asked for Susan's car and Susan had said that Celia could pay her for it at the end of the year, then that is valid consideration for the £750 that Celia pays Susan for the car. Similarly, in the *McArdle* case, if the family had asked the woman to carry out the work and told her that she would be paid, then her work would have been valid consideration.

Consideration from the promisee

The rule that consideration must 'move from the promisee' means that a person to whom a promise was made can only enforce it if he himself has provided the consideration. However, the promisee need not provide the whole consideration for the promise: thus he can enforce a promise, the consideration for which was provided partly by himself and partly by someone else acting as co-promisee. While consideration must move from the promisee, it need not move to the promisor. There can therefore be third-party consideration: for example, Joyce offers Bill £100 to repair Jamie's car. This would be a valid contract although Joyce does not receive the benefit of the consideration moving from Bill in return for her promise.

In some exceptional circumstances, the promisee (the receiver of the benefit of the promise) may confer a benefit on the promisor or on a third party without in fact suffering any detriment himself. If, for example, Marie-Lise promised Sunita £100 to repair Marie-Lise's car and Sunita gets her sister Farida to repair the car as a favour. In this example Sunita has suffered no tangible detriment. The essence of consideration should not therefore be thought to be the fact that the promisee suffers a detriment because this will not necessarily always be the case. An act, forbearance or promise will only amount to consideration if the law recognises that it has some economic value. In the above example Farida agrees with Sunita to fix Marie-Lise's car out of natural affection for her sister and her sister's friend. However, if Farida were to change her mind about fixing the car there would be no contract between her and Sunita to compel her to fix the car. Farida's reasons for promising to fix the car are merely sentimental and therefore unenforceable.

Illusory consideration

As well as having some economic value, consideration must not be illusory. In *White v Bluett* (1853), a son's promise not to bore his father with complaints was held not to be sufficient for a promise by the father to discharge the son's debts. A contemporary example would be if Garfield offers Brandon £30 to stop smoking for one week and Brandon has never smoked in his life and is in fact a puritanical anti-smoker then the consideration for the promise is entirely illusory. Contrast this situation to the situation where Brandon is a frequent smoker and Garfield shares a desk with him at work. In the latter scenario there is a situation where the promise provides an inducement to Brandon for his forbearance. This would be a valid contract even if Brandon had other reasons on his mind for wishing to stop his cigarette intake over the next week, for instance the perceived health benefits of so doing.

Consideration is also illusory where the promise alleged to be consideration leaves performance entirely at the whim of the promisor. However, such an arrangement can provide real consideration if a definite undertaking not to deal with any one else is included. Therefore an understanding from the manager of Tryall Golf Course to buy some golf balls from Del's Golf Ball Co at £6 per dozen can be readily distinguished from a contract for the manager of the golf course to buy all his golf balls from Del's Golf Ball Co.

Onerous gifts or collateral contracts as consideration

The reception of a gift of freehold or leasehold property can be valid consideration if the holding of such property is sufficiently onerous, for example a freehold property which is promised to someone if they promise to pay the outstanding mortgage and other charges can form the consideration for a binding agreement. A similar situation would be where Issac promises to give Lyn his leased flat if Lyn promises to fulfil Issac's repair and rent covenants under the lease. This agreement is binding as Issac has given away both his flat and his legal liabilities. He has received a benefit from Lyn for his promise of the flat.

Legal entitlements or liabilities as consideration

It is not surprising that a promise not to enforce a valid claim is clearly good consideration for a promise given in return. Legal liabilities or entitlement are of economic value and can form the consideration of a valid contract. Therefore promises not to enforce a claim or to abandon a good defence or to abandon a particular remedy can all amount to valid consideration; compare the decisions in the following cases: *The Leonidas D* (1985); *Banque de L'Indochine v JH Raymer (Mincing Lane) Ltd* (1983).

It cannot be valid consideration to provide a promise not to enforce a right which is worthless. If a claim is invalid because of its nature (for example, a gambling debt) then a promise to forbear from legal action in such connection is not and cannot be valid consideration. Similarly, a claim which the promisor knows is invalid or is clearly invalid cannot be the basis in law of good consideration. However, if there is doubt in law about the case then that can certainly be valid consideration because there is a possibility of benefit to one party or detriment to the other as the claim may well turn out to have been soundly based.

The courts have also held in certain circumstances that a promise not to pursue an invalid claim (ie that would fail at law) may constitute sufficient consideration for a promise to settle by the other party (*Callisher v Bischoffsheim* (1870)). The provisos that apply in this situation are that: the potential plaintiff has a *bona fide* belief in the prospect of his claim succeeding (*Horton v Horton* (1961) *(No 2)*); that he has made full and honest disclosure to the potential defendant of matters which might affect the validity of the claim (*Miles v NZ Alford Estate Co* (1886)); and he must show that he seriously intended to enforce the claim.

Forbearance

A person may forbear or refrain from enforcing a claim without expressly promising to do so. Where there is actual forbearance this may constitute consideration. In *Alliance Bank v Brown* the defendant owed the plaintiff bank some £22,000. The bank pressed him to give some security and he promised so to do but did not promise themselves not to sue him in the meantime. It was held that there was consideration for the defendant's promise as the bank had given, and the defendant had received 'some degree of forbearance'. A forbearance only amounts to consideration for a promise or performance that is induced by it. Where the forbearance is not requested expressly or by implication it is no consideration. In *Combe v Combe* (1951), a husband during divorce proceedings promised to pay his wife an annual allowance. In her action to enforce this promise one of the wife's arguments was that she had given consideration for it by forbearing to apply to the court for a maintenance order. The court rejected her argument holding that she had not forborne at her husband's request.

Performance of existing contractual duty

The general rule in this area is that where there is an existing contractual duty owed to the promisor by the promisee then mere performance of that duty by the promisee is not sufficient consideration for a new promise. Authority for this principle is the case of *Stilk v Myrick* which was reported in 1809. The facts of the case were that two sailors deserted a ship and the captain promised the remaining eight crew members extra wages if they would work the ship home to England. As they were already bound to do this under their original contracts it was held that the captain's promise was not binding. The recorded reasoning for this decision is twofold: first, that such promises could not be made enforceable as a matter of public policy because that would lead to extortion; and second, that the sailors provided no consideration by only doing what they were already bound to do. This second strand of reasoning has been subsequently followed.

Where there is a real factual benefit to the promisor and a real factual detriment to the promisee, then despite the pre-existence of contractual obligation a new contract may be validly formed. In *Hartley v Ponsonby* (1857), a case with a marked factual resemblance to the scenario in *Stilk v Myrick*, it was held that there was good consideration for the promise to pay extra wages. In that case the desertion of half the crew had effectively changed the nature of the return journey, as the fact that the ship was so thinly manned had significantly increased the peril of the voyage. The existing contractual authority had clearly been exceeded and effectively a fresh bargain had been entered into. The same principle was applied in the *Atlantic Baron* (1979) where shipbuilders claimed an increase in the agreed price for a supertanker on the basis that the payment currency stipulated had been devalued. The contract in that particular case also required the builders to give a performance guarantee and an increase in the performance guarantee was held to provide good consideration for the price increase.

In the Court of Appeal case of *Williams v Roffey and Nicholls* (1990) an important qualification to *Stilk v Myrick* was introduced whereby if the performance of an existing contractual duty confers a practical benefit on the promisor, this can constitute valid consideration. The facts of the case are that the contractors had engaged a carpentry sub-contractor, for the purpose of performing a contract between the contractors and the owners of a number of flats to refurbish the flats. The amount payable by the contractor to the sub-contractor was £20,000 but the contractor later promised to make extra payments to the sub-contractors. The sub-contractors made no new undertakings, indeed they did not solicit the extra payments as it was the contractors' own surveyor who recognised that the originally agreed sum was too low. The contractors feared that the sub-contractors (who were in financial difficulty) would not complete their portion of the work on time and so expose the contractors to penalties for delay under their contract with the owners of the flats.

Duties imposed by a contract with a third party

It is now accepted that actual performance of the promise to perform a contractual duty owed to a third party can constitute good consideration. In *Scotson v Pegg* (1861), Alpha agreed to deliver coal to Beta, or to Beta's order. Beta ordered Alpha to deliver the coal to Gamma. Gamma promised Alpha that if Alpha would deliver the coal that he would unload it. In an action brought by Alpha to try to enforce Gamma's promise, it was held that Alpha's delivery of the coal (the performance of an existing contractual duty to a third party) was good consideration to enforce Gamma's promise. Similarly in *The Eurymedon* (1938) a firm of stevedores unloaded goods from the ship. Some of the cargo belonged to a third party who had (effectively for the sake of this example) promised the ship's owners that they would not sue them. It was held by the Privy Council that the stevedores had provided consideration for this promise by unloading the cargo even if they were already bound by a valid contract with the owners of the ship to unload the ship anyway.

Further support for the rule is found in an extremely unusual domestic context in the case of *Shadwell v Shadwell* (1860). In this case an uncle wrote to his nephew stating that he was glad to hear of his intended marriage and that as he had promised him a start in married life that he would pay him £150 annually until he died. The majority of the Court of Common Pleas felt that the nephew had provided consideration for the uncle's promise by marrying his intended. It was suggested that there was a detriment to the nephew in that he 'may have made a most material change in his position, and induced the object of his affections to do the same and may have incurred pecuniary liabilities resulting in embarrassments'. It was also suggested that there was a real material benefit to the uncle in that the marriage was an object of interest to a near relative.

Part-payment of debt

The general common law rule is clear: a creditor is not bound by an undertaking to accept part payment in full settlement of a debt. An accrued debt can only be discharged by full accord and satisfaction. A promise by a debtor to pay a proportion of his debt provides no consideration for an enforceable agreement as such an agreement is without more merely a promise to perform a pre-existing contractual duty. The common law rule was established in *Pinnel's* case (1602). As well as the rule that the part-payment of a debt is not good consideration for a promise to forgo the balance it was also held in *Pinnel's* case that a creditor's agreement to accept part-payment would be binding if at the creditor's request the debtor provided some new consideration (for example by accepting payment early, or by accepting payment in goods or by accepting payment in a different country or in a different currency).

The principle in *Pinnel's* case was affirmed by the House of Lords in *Foakes v Beer* (1884) and despite its lack of commercial reality still represents the law. There are three common law exceptions to the rule: where a creditor's claim is uncertain either because it is disputed in good faith or because it is for an unliquidated sum; where there has been part-payment by a third party; or where there is a composition agreement in place. The rationale for the first exception is that where a commodity is of uncertain value and there remains the possibility (strong or not) of the creditor in the end receiving less than the value of the debtor's offer as his legal entitlement, the court will not intervene to judge the adequacy of the consideration on offer in any new contract. The second exception comes about because if part-payment by a third party is accepted by the creditor as full and final settlement of the debtor's liability, it would be tantamount to permitting the court to be used as the instrument of fraud to allow the creditor to break the perfectly valid contract he or she holds with the third party by pursuing the debtor for full satisfaction of the debt, cf *Welby v Drake* (1825). In the third situation a debtor who cannot pay all his creditors in full may be able to induce them to agree with himself and such others to accept a dividend as full settlement of their claims. A creditor who has accepted a dividend under such an agreement cannot sue the debtor for the balance of his original demand. If the debtor fails to pay the agreed dividend, then the original debt revives, otherwise the creditor is bound by the new agreement, cf *Wood v Roberts* (1818). The reason for this rule is again a matter of policy as the courts will not be party to any individual creditor seeking to profit by breaking his agreement with the others.

Promissory estoppel

In addition to those common law limitations to the *Pinnel's* rule, there is a further and controversial equitable limitation. It is called the doctrine of promissory estoppel and it creates a method of making a promise which is binding in certain circumstances in the absence of consideration. This modern equitable doctrine is thought to rest largely on the judicial intervention of Denning J in the *Central London Property Trust v High Trees House Ltd* (1947) and on a 1955 House of Lords decision in *Tool Metal Manufacturing Co Ltd v Tungsten Electric Co Ltd* (1955). However, the doctrine's genesis can be traced back to the House of Lords decision in *Hughes v Metropolitan Railway* (1877). In that case the landlord gave his tenant six months to repair the premises, it being clear that in the event of the tenant's failure to repair the premises that the lease would be forfeited. Within the six months, the landlord opened discussions with his tenant for the sale of the lease. During these discussions the tenant carried out no repairs on the premises. After the negotiations between the landlord and the tenant broke down and after the original six months had expired the landlord claimed the forfeiture of the lease. The House of Lords held that the landlord could not so do, as the landlord had, by his conduct, led his tenant to think that the landlord would not enforce forfeiture at the end of the notice period and the tenant had relied on this by not carrying out the repairs. The House of Lords therefore found that the six month notice period would only start to run again from the date on which the negotiations between the landlord and the tenant had floundered and broken down.

The rationale behind the *Hughes* case was in effect a form of equitable estoppel which could arise from a promise as to future conduct or intention unlike common law estoppel which relies on a representation as to existing fact. Thus equitable estoppel is 'promissory' estoppel. *Hughes v Metropolitan Railway* was relied on in the *High Trees* case. Here the landlords of a block of flats agreed to accept half the ground rent stipulated in the lease from the tenants because the wartime conditions had led, *inter alia*, to a lack of subtenants. Denning J held that by the end of the war the landlords were entitled to the full rent as the circumstances which gave rise to the rent reduction were no longer in existence. The judge then went on to say, despite the lack of any consideration in the case, that if the landlords had attempted to recover the balance of the rent that fell due over the war years (when only half the rent was paid) in his view the landlords would have been estopped from so doing in equity.

Promissory estoppel is a defensive doctrine. It may be used by promisees as a shield from inequitable writs or statements of claim but it cannot be used as a cause of action in its own right, cf *Combe v Combe* (1951). Hence the doctrine does not dispense with the requirement of consideration in the creation of valid contracts. This equitable estoppel operates: where there has been a clear and unambiguous representation by the promisor that they will not enforce their strict legal rights against the promisee; and the promisee must then have acted in reliance on the promise (this will usually be to the detriment of the promisee although in *W J Alan Co Ltd v El Nasr Export and Import* (1972) Lord Denning MR suggested that any specific action in reliance would do); and finally, it must be inequitable for the promisor to go back their word by striving to revive their strict legal rights.

In *Tool Metal Manufacturing Co Ltd v Tungsten Electric Co Ltd* the patent owners promised to suspend periodic payments of compensation due to them from manufacturers from the outbreak of war. The House of Lords held that the promise was binding during the period of suspension, but the owners could, on giving reasonable notice to the other party, revert to their legal entitlement to receive the compensation payments. This case has been frequently followed in the Court of Appeal and in the case of *Alan v El Nasr*, Lord Denning MR restated the doctrine thus, that:

> the one who waives his strict rights cannot afterwards insist on them. His strict rights are at any rate suspended so long as the waiver lasts. He may on occasion be able to revert to his strict legal rights for the future by giving reasonable notice in that behalf , or making it plain by his conduct that he will thereafter insist on them ... But there are cases where no withdrawal is possible. It may be too late to withdraw; or it cannot be done without injustice to the other party. In that event he will be bound by his waiver. He can only enforce them subject to the waiver he has made.

The House of Lords is, however, yet to rule which cases fit these latter categories and it is therefore not clear whether promissory estoppel is merely suspensive of the rights of the promisor to full payment or whether it is capable of being exhaustive of those rights.

The factual analysis: opinion writing

Here is a case scenario which seeks to highlight some of the legal issues addressed in this chapter.

CASE SCENARIO

Counsel is instructed by Dobb and Co and has herewith the statement of Mr Lindburgh Wormes, Managing Director of Corelco Co Ltd, Surrey. Memorandum from Cherry Tree Co Ltd, the Shopfitters' Association, evidencing the agreement to pay £200,000 if works are completed on schedule.

Counsel will gather the details from the statement of Mr Linburgh Wormes; but briefly, Corelco Co Ltd are unhappy, after having agreed to accept the contract between themselves and Cherry Tree Association as discharged, now feel that they have a claim to the rest of the sweetener they were promised. Counsel is instructed to advise generally on the strength of the case in Corelco's favour and the likelihood of success.

The practical approach

The first step is to identify the relevant factual and legal issues.

Legal and factual issues

- Is Cherry Tree Co Ltd's promise of £200,000 enforceable by Corelco Co Ltd?

- Has Corelco Co Ltd given any or any sufficient consideration to Cherry Tree Co Ltd by meeting their original deadline?

- Is it of any significance that the works are completed ahead of schedule?

- What is the legal status of Corelco's acceptance of a lesser amount together with the discount vouchers? Is it a discharge of Cherry Tree Co Ltd's contractual obligation?

- What is the legal status of the discount vouchers?

- Can Corelco Co Ltd be stopped?

- What loss has Corelco suffered as a result of the purported breach?

- What remedies if any are open to Corelco Co Ltd?

Dramatis personae

- Corelco Co Ltd: Construction Company;

- Cherry Tree Co Ltd – representing the shopfitters' association;

- Duncombe Ltd: the contractors/development company.

Gaps in instructions: to be requested

Any gaps or ambiguities generally relate to the missing evidence and although counsel is not able to advise completely on the basis of the evidence before him, he must do his best to advise on the available evidence anticipating any expected piece of evidence from the other side, and how it would alter his view of his client's success.

- Evidence of any loss suffered by Corelco Co Ltd;
- Evidence of any reliance placed by Corelco on Cherry Tree Co Ltd's promise;
- Evidence of the discharge of Corelco Co Ltd of its agreement with Cherry Tree Co Ltd;
- Copy of contracts between Corelco Co Ltd and Cherry Tree Co Ltd and Duncombe Ltd;
- Copies of all correspondence, and notes, memoranda of all conversations between Corelco Co Ltd and Cherry Tree Co Ltd.

Statement by Mr Lindburgh Wormes, Managing Director of Corelco Co Ltd

I am the Managing Director of Corelco Co Ltd, a construction company specialising in commercial premises. Under the terms of a written contract dated 15 August 1994, the company agreed with Duncombe Ltd to build a parade of up-market shops in Kings Plaza, Oval. It was agreed that the works on the Plaza Complex were to be completed by 19 December 1994 at a price of £3.5 million.

The Plaza was to consist of six shops: a specialist confectionery, a gift shop, a perfumery, a patisserie, a lingerie boutique and a luggage shop. The development company stipulated that expensive Italian tiles should be used to pave the main area to the parade. Our tile suppliers in Rome notified us that there was a possibility that perhaps because of the summer there was a risk that there could be some delay in getting the amount of tiles to the company by the due date. There was a possibility that we would not meet a scheduled deadline as per the contract. We notified Duncombe Ltd, the contractors, that there was a likelihood that the building works would be late and perhaps not be completed until the new year.

The development company told the shopfitters' association, the association responsible for renting the shops, of this possible delay. The company, who were represented by a company called Cherry Tree Co Ltd, approached me and promised to pay our company £200,000 out of expected profits if the complex was opened on time. The profits they said were to come from the Christmas opening and from a special Christmas charity function which was being held at the Oval. They expected massive takings as a result of the spin-off from the

27

charity events which would attract many popular artists. As things turned out the tiles arrived on time and we were able to complete the work ahead of schedule, in fact by 9 December.

In February 1995 Cherry Tree Co Ltd wrote to me enclosing a cheque for £100,000, and some 15% discount vouchers for shopping at all the shops in the parade. At a company meeting the directors agreed that we should accept £100,000 and the vouchers and regard the contract as terminated between ourselves and the shopfitters association. However, we have just learned that the Plaza is to host the May Day Champagne Ball and the shops would be open all day and all night. The new contract is worth over £300,000 to Cherry Tree Co Ltd. The directors feel that in the circumstances we should now claim the outstanding amount of £100,000 originally promised to our company.

THE OPINION

Corelco Co Ltd and Cherry Tree Co Ltd

1 I am asked to advise Corelco Ltd as to what, if any, remedies are available to them against Cherry Tree Co Ltd. Corelco Co Ltd had a contract with Duncombe Ltd to complete six shops by 9 December. Cherry Tree Co Ltd, the shopfitters' association, and the company responsible for renting the shops, offered Corelco Co Ltd the sum of £200,000 if the building works were completed by the due date. This money was to be paid from expected profits from pre-Christmas and a Christmas Gala held in the Plaza. Corelco Co in fact finished the work ahead of schedule. Corelco accepted a payment of £100,000 and discount vouchers in complete discharge of the debt. It is subsequently learned that a large contract was won by Cherry Tree Co Ltd and as a result Corelco Ltd feel that they should be paid the outstanding £100,000.

2 The enforceability of Cherry Tree Co Ltd's promise

The main issue here is whether Corelco Co can enforce the promise made by Cherry Tree Co Ltd by insisting on the additional £100,000 being paid. The legal question is: has Corelco Co provided sufficient or any consideration by completing the works on schedule? The major problem is that Corelco Co were already under a pre-existing contractual duty to Duncombe Ltd to complete these works. The difficulty I am faced with is finding any detriment alleged to have been suffered by Corelco as a result of the loss of the £100,000 which they accepted. It is clear that this secondary contract with Cherry Tree Co Ltd does not in any way affect the main contract with Duncombe Ltd. It is arguable that some evidence of detriment could be the reliance Corelco placed on the promise to complete the works early. The concern I have with this is that the completion of the works early was not something intrinsic to the contract and was not in fact a term of the contract with Cherry Tree Co Ltd. I am bound to say that on the face of it, I cannot see that Corelco has suffered any detriment as they are already bound to render the performance of completion to Duncombe Ltd. It is clear, however, despite this argument that even without considering this aspect a valid contract does exist between Corelco and Cherry Tree Co Ltd based on the duty owed to a third party, ie Duncombe Ltd and it is a contract which is *prima facie* enforceable.

3 Agreement to accept the £100,000 binding on Corelco Co Ltd

Corelco Co Ltd had agreed to accept £100,000 and discount shopping vouchers in place of £200,000. The question is whether this agreement is binding on them as a contract supported by consideration. The general rule is that part-payment of a lesser sum is not satisfaction for the whole debt except where there have been agreed changes in how the debt should be discharged or the addition of something new which the law regards as having value. This then would amount to sufficient consideration for the creditor's promise not to press for further payment of the debt due to him. It is clear on this argument that Cherry Tree Co Ltd still owes Corelco Ltd £100,000. The question now is: do the discount shopping vouchers represent something of value and did Corelco, in return for these vouchers, promise Cherry Tree Co Ltd to extinguish the debt on receipt of them. My instructions here are less than clear. I would be grateful if instructing solicitors could obtain a further and more detailed statement from Mr Wormes regarding this point. It is my view that if there had been an explicit undertaking on Corelco's part not to proceed, then the matter can be taken no further. However, had there been no such promise, the giving of shopping vouchers would amount to no consideration or at best past consideration and would allow Corelco to pursue its action for the outstanding balance.

4 Duress

I am not told the circumstances of how the reduced amount came to be offered and accepted, except that there was a letter of apology. Were there any follow-up conversations between the parties and, if so, what was the content of such conversations? This information is useful to help me determine whether Cherry Tree Co Ltd exerted any pressure on Corelco which forced them to accept the lesser amount. Could instructing solicitors kindly ask Mr Wormes to address the question of the contents of the conversation in his additional statement, as this could change the complexion of the whole matter?

5 Finally it is my opinion taking a very preliminary view that subject to what information I receive in Mr Wormes' additional statement and other additional evidence, there may be a case worth pursuing on behalf of Corelco Co Ltd. I put my opinion no higher than this at present, since I yet await these further details. However, I have drafted a statement of claim and instructing solicitors will find it attached herewith.

14 September 1995

B A Barrister
7 Kings Court
Chancery Lane
London W11

IN THE HIGH COURT OF JUSTICE   1995

BETWEEN

Corelco Co Ltd   *Plaintiffs*

and

Cherry Tree Co Ltd   *Defendants*

STATEMENT OF CLAIM

1   The plaintiffs were and are at all material times a construction company, the defendants, a shopfitter's managing company.

2   By an oral contract dated ... the defendants agreed to pay the plaintiffs £200,000 on the completion of certain building works.

3   Upon completion of said works the defendants paid £100,000 and have refused complete payment of balance thereof, namely £100,000 which remains due and owing to them.

4   By virtue of the matters aforesaid the plaintiffs have lost the revenue they would otherwise have received under the agreement and have suffered loss and damage.

Particulars of loss

    (a)

    (b)

    (c)

5   And the plaintiffs claim interest pursuant to section 35A of the Supreme Court Act 1981 upon such sums as for such amounts and the plaintiffs claim:

    (i)   The said sum of £100,000

    (ii) Damages for repudiation of the said agreement

    (iii) Interest

B A Barrister
8 Kings Bench Walk
Temple
WC1R

4   Terms of the contract

Introduction

The actual content of any particular contract depends on the statements made by the contracting parties as they entered into their agreement. Those words make up the express terms of the contract between them. A contract may in addition contain terms which while not expressly stated are implied, either because the parties so intended, or by custom or usage of the operation of the law. All the terms of a contract whether express or implied, determine the extent of each party's rights and duties under the contract.

The express terms of a contract consist of those representations made by the parties to one another during the negotiation which led to the formation of the contract in question and by which they intended to be bound. To discover which representations and statements the parties wished to enshrine as terms of their contract, the court will have to examine the words and ask what a reasonable man would understand the intention of the parties to be, having regard to all the circumstances. This is an objective test of agreement and under it, one party cannot seek to enforce a contract according to his subjective view of its content, if his view and the sense that he gives to the words differ from the sense that the court determines should reasonably be given to the statements.

Certainty

In some circumstances the words exchanged by the parties as they entered into their agreement are so vague that when looked at objectively no definite meaning can be give without the addition of a number of new terms. The courts will not do this. In *Scammell v Ouston* (1941) the House of Lords decided that an agreement to buy a car on hire-purchase was not a contract that could be enforced. Given the huge number of different types of hire-purchase agreements, it was impossible to say on which terms the parties intended to contract. It is not the role of the courts to substitute its intention for that of the parties in order to prevent a contract being declared void.

However, it remains the case that the courts will always strike down a contract which is not drafted with the utmost skill and precision. If in a particular instance there is an established trade usage or custom to which reference can be had to explain an ostensibly vague or incomplete agreement by the parties, then the courts will have recourse to it. In *Hillas v Arcos* (1932) the House of Lords did not strike down an agreement made by persons familiar with the conventions of the timber trade for the sale of timber of 'fair specification.' It is commercial reality that in some long-term situations the parties to an agreement may be reluctant to tie themselves to rigid arrangements, particularly when factors affecting performance and price are likely to fluctuate. In *Foley v Classique Coaches* (1934) the plaintiff was the owner of a petrol station and the adjoining land. He sold the land to Classique Coaches Ltd on condition that they should enter into an agreement to buy petrol for the purpose of their motor coach business exclusively from him. This agreement was formalised into a contract, but the defendant company broke it and sought to argue that the agreement was incomplete and therefore not binding because it provided that the petrol should be bought from the petrol station 'at a price agreed by the parties from time to time'. The Court of Appeal rejected this argument and held that in default of agreement a reasonable price should be paid.

The courts are concerned, especially when parties have acted on agreements, to avoid striking down contracts which contain superfluous meaningless clauses. In *Nicolene v Simmonds* (1953), a contract for the sale of steel bars contained a term which stated 'I assume ... that the usual conditions of acceptance apply.' There were, however, no usual conditions of acceptance and so the other terms of the contract being certain the Court of Appeal had little difficulty excising the offending term. Similarly, the courts are equally hesitant to strike down a contract where there is a mechanism for resolving the matter left open in the agreement. The courts will even go so far as to 'repair' the mechanism as long as the nature of the breakdown is relatively minor. Hence in *Sudbrook Trading Estate v Eggleton* (1983) a lease gave the tenant the option to purchase the premises at such price as may be agreed by two valuers, one to be nominated by each party. The landlord attempted to frustrate the option by refusing to appoint a valuer. The House of Lords held that the option did not fail for uncertainty. The contract between the parties on its true construction amounted to an agreement to sell at a reasonable price to be determined by the valuers; and the the requirement that each party should nominate one of the valuers was clearly 'subsidiary and inessential'.

Parol evidence

The terms of a contract may be contained in more than one document, for example many employment contracts are made subject to professional codes of conduct by reference. These codes and disciplinary rules are then part of the totality of the contract. The parol evidence rule is a general rule of evidence but it applies to contract law to ensure that where a contract is embodied in a written document then extrinsic evidence is not admissible to add, vary, subtract from, or contradict the evidence of the written document. This rule does not conflict with the ability to incorporate other documents by reference to them in the agreement; however, the rule does act to prevent contracting parties relying on evidence which is extrinsic to both documents, ie the whole contract.

The parol evidence rule as it applies to contracts is convenient as it promotes certainty by ensuring that what parties who have reduced a contract into writing should be bound by is the writing and the writing alone. The rule provides a sound basis for the court to attempt to objectively construe the intention of the parties and the terms of the contract in the event of dispute between the contracting parties. On the other hand, the rule excludes such material that would otherwise be deemed relevant, such as draft contracts and correspondence. This is a problem where a document looks like a complete contract when it does not in fact accurately reflect some aspect of the agreement between the parties. In this situation the party who relies on the document does not have to prove that he had the belief that the document seems to indicate, he can rely on a presumption to that effect which it is up to the objecting party to rebut. See the case of *Walker Property Investments Ltd v Walker* (1947). The danger of the rule is that its presumption is based purely on the nature and form of the document, rather than on an inquiry about the actual belief of the parties as to whether that document formed the totality of the contract.

As a result of this problem the Law Commission has recommended the abolition of the rule and over the years a variety of ways have been devised to circumvent it to varying degrees. The rule only prevents a party from relying on extrinsic evidence as to the contents of the contract, and not as to its validity. Extrinsic evidence is admissible to show that the contract is invalid for mistake, misrepresentation, incapacity or lack of consideration. Extrinsic evidence is also admissible to show that the contract has not yet come into operation or conversely that it has ceased to operate. In *Pym v Campbell* (1856) there was a written agreement for the sale of a share in a patent. The parties orally agreed that the agreement was not to operate until a third party had approved the invention. Evidence of the oral agreement was admitted. Extrinsic evidence is also permissible to show the customs of a locality or trade usage but when this is done the new evidence cannot contradict the written agreement, only add to it.

Representations

It is in the nature of contractual negotiations that each side will make a number of verbal and/or written statements. As a result of these negotiations agreement will be reached. The status of these statements will become crucial because they determine the remedies available should the statements relied on prove false or an implied promise be broken. For example, if Jo wishes to sell her motorbike to Liz, their final agreement may well be concluded in these terms: Will you accept £800 for the bike? Yes. This will frequently not be the full extent of the agreement between the parties. Earlier Jo may have told Liz that this is the 1993 model; that it is a nice bike; that it has a chain drive; that she has only used it on

Sundays; and that she has regularly serviced the bike, etc. By making such representations Jo will know that she may have induced Liz's offer, indeed that would have probably been her intention. If any of Jo's statements turn out to be false once Liz has bought the bike, then it will have to be determined whether Jo's representations were merely vague advertising claims; representations which if false may form the basis of a claim of misrepresentation; or a term of the contract which if broken will allow a remedy for breach. The difficulty in this area is that one cannot tell a term from a representation merely by looking at the words used. It is necessary to clarify what the parties said according to the circumstances in which they said it. The effect of Jo's words could be very different if she is a specialist motorcycle dealer or, indeed, for that matter if Liz is a specialist motorcycle dealer.

Trade puffs

These are statements which are nothing more than vague advertising claims. They have no effect in contract. In *Lambert v Lewis* (1981), a manufacturer claimed in his promotional material that his product was foolproof and that it required no maintenance. These statements were held not to be a term of a contract between manufacturer and dealer (who, incidentally, had not bought the product directly from the manufacturer anyway). It was held that these comments were 'not intended to be, nor were they acted on as being express warranties'. However, where a more precise claim is made in promotional literature such as a claim that my smoke ball will prevent the contraction of influenza (*Carbolic Smoke Ball v Carlill*). A distinction must be drawn between the former indiscriminate praise and specific claims or assertions of verifiable facts.

Representations

A representation is a statement which induces the contract but does not form part of it. An assertion such as the one that occurred in *Bissett v Wilkinson* (1927), that a piece of land would be able to support 2,000 sheep was held to be a mere statement of opinion. Such a statement of belief will be merely a representation unless a party has or is regarded to have some special knowledge or skill as to the matter stated.

Terms

A term is a promise or undertaking which is part of the contract itself. Whether a statement is a representation or a term is primarily a question of intention. In the case of a written contract, if the parties indicate in the document that a statement is to be regarded as a term then the court will usually implement their wish. In all other cases, the parties' intention has to be objectively ascertained and while it is impossible to lay strict rules as to how you find the parties' intention, guidelines over the years have been unofficially created such as: a statement is unlikely to be a term of the contract if the person making it expressly asks the other party to verify its truth; a statement is likely to be a term of the contract where its importance is such that if it had not been made, the representee would not have entered into the contract at all; and a statement's classification may depend on the relative capacities of the parties.

Verification

A statement is unlikely to be a term of the contract if the person making the statement asks the other party to check and verify it. This is illustrated by the case of *Ecay v Godfrey* (1947): the seller of a boat stated that it was sound but advised the buyer to have it surveyed. However, if the statement is made with the intention of preventing the other party from finding a defect and this has the effect that it induces the other party to contract in reliance on the statement, then the courts will hold that that statement is a term of the contract. In *Schawel v Reade* (1912) the purchaser of a horse, who was just about to examine the animal, was told not to examine the horse because it was perfectly sound. The buyer then bought the horse without examination, relying on this statement. The horse was not sound and the House of Lords found that the statement was a term.

Importance of a term

Where it is clear that the injured party or plaintiff would not have entered into the contract had the statement not been made, then again the statement is a term. The leading case in this area is *Bannerman v White* (1861), where an intending buyer of hops asked specifically whether they had been treated with sulphur, saying that it they had he would not even trouble to ask the price. The seller erroneously assured him they had not been treated with sulphur and the Court of Appeal held that this was a term.

Special skill

A statement may be assessed by the court to be a term when one of the parties possesses superior skill and knowledge relating to the subject matter of the contract. In *Oscar Chess Ltd v Williams* (1957), the seller was a private car owner who made the innocent misrepresentation (when attempting to part-exchange his car) that the car was a 1948 model when in fact it was a 1938 model. The Court of Appeal held that the statement as to the age of the car was not a term but a representation as the buyers, being car dealers, were in just as strong a position as the seller to verify the truth of the statement. By contrast, a car dealer gave a false statement as to the mileage of a Bentley motor car in *Dick Bentley Production Ltd v Harold Smith (Motors) Ltd* (1965). In this case the car dealer was clearly in a better position than the buyer to know whether the representation was true, and the Court of Appeal held this to be a warranty. A statement of opinion by some-one who has special skill may be a term where the opinion states a fact which is difficult ordinarily to verify. In *Leaf v International Galleries* (1950), the Court of Appeal indicated that a representation made that a picture was a Constable could be a warranty.

Collateral contract

In the case where a contract is entered into on the strength of a statement made by one of the contracting parties, there may be a secondary or 'collateral' con-tract based on those words. To take effect as a collateral contract it is necessary for the statement: to have been intended to have contractual effect (like the statements forming the main contract); and there must be some indication that the parties intended the statement to take effect as a collateral contract and not simply as a term in the main contract. In *Mann v Nunn* (1874) the plaintiff tenant agreed to take a lease of the defendant landlord's premises, if the landlord would first do certain repairs. A written agreement was later executed, but did not refer to the defendant's promise to do the repairs. Nevertheless the tenant was still able to enforce the promise. There is a risk that the collateral contract often serves no purpose but to avoid the strictures of the parole evidence rule as a collateral contract may be valid even though it conflicts with a term in the main contract (*City of Westminster Properties Ltd v Mudd* (1959)). Therefore, 'col-lateral contracts the sole effect is to vary or add to the terms of the principal con-tract are therefore viewed with suspicion by the law': Lord Moulton in *Heilbut, Symons and Co v Buckleton*. This is despite the fact that the court will not find such a contract unless all the elements of a separate valid contract are present.

Conditions, warranties and terms

The traditional distinction between terms in contract law has always been between conditions and warranties (although we shall see that this is not any longer strictly true). A condition is an important term in a contract. A term that is so important that its breach is sufficient to allow the wronged party the right to rescind the contract. A warranty, however, is a term the breach of which gives the wronged party only a right to damages.

If a particular contractual term relates to a substantial ingredient in the iden-tity of the contract, that is the performance of the term's stipulation goes to the root of the contract, then it will be classed as a condition. The theory is that it would be unjust to pay for something which differed in an important way from that for which he had contracted. A warranty, on the other hand, concerns some less important or subsidiary element of the contract, breach of which can be adequately remedied by the payment of money.

Express classification by the contracting parties

A term may be classified as a condition either by the express agreement of the parties or by law. (In some cases, there is statutory intervention as well as judicial, eg Sale of Goods Act 1979 ss 12–15.) If a contract expressly says that a particular term is a condition, that term will generally be so regarded. The same is also true generally where the contract expressly states that rescission will be available on breach of the statement. However, in cases where a term is given the title 'condition' in the contractual document, the court will still examine the contract to ascertain that it was the parties' intention that breach of that term should justify rescission. Where it is apparent that such a term could be breached and cause either minimal or no loss, then the court may hold that such a breach does not justify rescission, as the House of Lords held in *Wickman Machine Tool Sales v Schuler AG* (1973).

Technical breaches

There is, however, also House of Lords authority for the proposition that 'there are many cases ... where terms the breaches of which do not deprive the innocent party of substantially the whole benefit which he was intended to receive from the contract were nonetheless held to be conditions which entitled the innocent party to rescind' (Lord Roskill *Bunge Corp v Tradax Export SA* (1981)). In *Arcos v Ronaasen* (1933) this was exactly the case. Timbers were bought for the purpose of making cement barrels and were described in the contract as half an inch thick. In fact most of the timber delivered was in fact nine-sixteenths of an inch thick and, although this did not in the least impair its usefulness for making cement barrels, it was held that the buyers were nevertheless entitled to reject it.

Innominate terms

The courts' concern at parties to contract being able to use the most technical and trivial deficiencies in conditions of contracts which have become bad because of changes to the market price has been expressed in an increased tendency to reduce the number of terms classified as conditions. In the Hongkong *Fir Shipping Co Ltd v Kawaski Kisen Kaisha Ltd* (1962) case Diplock LJ recognised that there are contractual undertakings which cannot be categorised as being conditions or warranties:

> of such undertakings all that can be predicated is that some breaches will and others will
> not give rise to an event which will deprive the party not in default of substantially the

39

whole benefit of which it was intended that he should obtain.

These innominate terms differ from conditions in that breach does not of itself necessarily give rise to a right to rescind; and they differ from warranties in that the wronged party's remedy is not even *prima facie* restricted to damages. The wronged or injured party can rescind for the breach of an innominate term but only if the requirement of substantial failure is satisfied. The availability of this remedy is demonstrated by the case of *Federal Commerce and Navigation v Molena Alpha* (1978) where a time charter had authorised the charterer to sign bills of lading stating that freight had been prepaid. Despite this the shipowners wrongfully withdrew that authority and instructed the captain to sign bills of lading only in a form that was commercially useless to the charterer. It was held that although the term broken was not actually condition, the result was to deprive the charterer of the virtually the whole benefit of the contract. Hence it followed that the charterer was entitled to rescind.

While not trying to mitigate from the position that contracting parties should be bound to perform the conditions that they freely agree to at the time pre-scribed by the contract, the courts have moved to a situation where they are not overly ready to construe terms as conditions unless the contract clearly requires the court to do so. Lord Wilberforce in *Bunge v Tradax* has expressly approved the view that the court should not be too ready to interpret contractual clauses as conditions. The state of the law therefore appears to be that: where terms are sufficiently precise and if performance of each of them is commercially vital; or there is evidence either from the commercial setting; or from the negotiations that the contracting parties intended the terms to have the force of conditions, then the courts will deem the terms to be conditions. In other cases the courts will not be too hasty to classify a term as a condition and it is instead likely to be classified as an intermediate term (with the result that rescission will only be allowed when the breach causes very serious prejudice to the wronged party).

Implied terms

There are three ways in which terms that are not expressly stated in the parties' agreement may be implied into their contract: statute; the officious bystander test; and custom.

Statute

The most important statute in this regard is the Sale of Goods Act 1979. Section 14 implies that where goods are sold in the course of a business then those goods shall be of merchantable quality and reasonably fit for the purpose for which they are required. Section 12 creates the implied condition that: the goods are free from encumbrances; that the buyer will enjoy quiet possession; and that the seller has a right to sell the goods. Section 13 provides an implied term that the goods will correspond with their description (or their sample, where there is a sale by sample s 15).

Officious bystander test

> An implied warranty ... as distinguished from an express contract or express warranty, really is in every instance founded on the presumed intention of the parties and upon reason.
>
> Lord Justice Bowen, *The Moorcock.*

The parties must both have intended to include the implied term in order to give the contract efficacy. It is not enough for the term sought to be implied merely to be reasonable *(Liverpool CC v Irwin* (1976)). It must be so obvious that if while the parties were negotiating an officious bystander were to suggest that they make this an express term they would suppress him with a common, 'Oh, of course' *(Shirlaw v Southern Foundries Ltd* (1939)).

In *The Moorcock* (1889) the defendant wharf owners came to an agreement to allow *The Moorcock* to be unloaded on their wharf. However, as the tide dipped, the ship grounded and sustained damage on the river bed. In the absence of an express term to take reasonable care that the mooring was safe, the defendants were held liable under an implied term that was necessary to give the contract efficacy.

Custom

Trade usage and local custom may assist the courts to imply terms into a contract on matters in which the agreement is silent *(Hutton v Warren* (1836)).

The factual analysis: opinion writing

Again what follows in this section is a case scenario which attempts to incorporate some of the legal issues covered in this chapter.

CASE SCENARIO

Counsel is instructed by Dobb and Co Solicitors who have been approached by Mavis Foote, a renowned ragga singer, part of a singing trio called 'The Moves'. Counsel will find herewith a statement by Miss Foote and a relevant extract from her entertainment contract with Virgo Plus Ltd, The Moves' promotions agent. Counsel is asked to advise Miss Foote.

In essence the facts are: Mavis Foote agreed as did the other members of The Moves to sing as backup only to Herman Starr, and to wear gowns manufactured only by Virgo Plus Ltd. The Moves together with Herman Starr were to perform at the Sevenoaks outdoor arena. On the night of the performance the two other members of the trio became ill with chickenpox and were unable to perform. Miss Foote accepted an invitation to appear as a solo artiste in their place. She mistakenly wore a costume designed by Sinco Ltd. Virgo Plus has informed her that her contract has been repudiated, because of her breach.

The practical approach

Legal and factual issues

- What are the terms of the contract? How certain are they?

- Virgo Plus are purporting to repudiate the contract, therefore the distinction between condition warranty/in nominate term is important.

- Is the term 'not to sing except' a condition which goes to the root of the contract?

- Has the second term 'only to wear gowns manufactured by Virgo Plus Ltd' been broken?

- Are both terms reasonable under the circumstances?

- Could a term be implied that Mavis Foote should be free to perform solo, as long as she did not sing?

- Does Mavis Foote have any defences?

- What is the strength of her case?

- Could Sinco Ltd bring a separate action against Mavis Foote for misrepresentation – ie that they were her promotions agent?

Dramatis personae

- Mavis Foote – putative defendant in an action for breach of contract;

- Virgo Plus Ltd – putative plaintiff – alleging breach of contract, and assuming the right to rescind the employment contract between themselves and Mavis Foote;

- Sinco Ltd – possible plaintiff in an action against Mavis Foote;

- Megan Zoss – possible third party – Mavis Foote may consider joining her in respect of liability in regards to the issue of wearing Sinco Ltd's dress.

Gaps in instructions: to be requested

- Complete copy of Mavis Foote's contract with Virgo Plus Ltd;

- A copy of the tape of the performance on 6 July 1994;

- Copies of any correspondence between Virgo Plus Ltd and, if any, Sinco Ltd and also from Megan Zoss.

Extract of contract of employment between M Foote and Virgo Ltd

Mavis Foote accepted the following terms of the contract:

- Not to sing in any event except as part of the group, The Moves;

- To only wear gowns manufactured and supplied by Virgo Plus Ltd.

Statement by Mavis Ann Foote of 7 The Willows, Farneham, Kent

I have been part of The Moves group for the past six years. We are the backup singing group to Herman Starr. We are all promoted and managed by Virgo Plus Ltd. The terms of the contract do not allow us to sing for anyone else except Virgo Plus Ltd, and while performing only to wear the gowns provided by the company.

On 6 July 1994, everyone in the dressing room suddenly began to cough and great blotches appeared on their skins. The doctor was called and it turned out that everyone had chickenpox, except me. As I was leaving the dressing room, Megan Zoss, the show promoter, came up to me and asked me whether I could oblige by filling in the spot left by Herman Starr and The Moves, as a solo artiste.

Thinking that I was helping out Virgo Plus Ltd, who may have had to pay Megan Zoss for cancelling, I agreed. It suddenly occurred to me that the make-up artist had taken away my Virgo Plus costume; Miss Zoss said she had another Virgo costume left behind from our last show. I did not doubt her and wore the costume provided. I performed three numbers, not singing, but stand-up comedy acts which included singing a few lines in impersonations. As I changed I noticed that the label in the dress was Sinco Ltd, Virgo Plus's biggest rival in promotions. I asked Miss Zoss about this and she apologised and said that it was a mistake. She thought the costume had been a Virgo dress. Virgo Plus have now repudiated my contract and said that I am in breach.

THE OPINION

Re: Mavis Foote

1 I am asked to advise Miss Foote, whose entertainment contract as a backup singer with The Moves has been purportedly repudiated by Virgo Plus Ltd, her promoter and agent. It seems that *prima facie* Miss Foote has breached the terms of her contract, (i) 'not to sing in any event except as part of The Moves', (ii) 'to only wear gowns manufactured and supplied by Virgo Plus Ltd'.

2 Term one – contract or warranty

It seems quite clear that the two clauses Miss Foote has allegedly breached are terms of the contract. The important issue is how these terms should be classified, as this will determine whether Virgo Plus Ltd will in fact be entitled to repudiate the contract if they can show that Miss Foote is in breach.

The initial question is whether this term is a condition, and, if it is, does it go to the root of the contract between the parties? Without evidence of what it is that the term is intended to prohibit, the question is difficult to answer. However, it does seem clear that the agreement is about Miss Foote singing as part of The Moves. It would appear that the basis of the contract was to prohibit any member of The Moves from singing as a solo artiste and that any other form of entertainment by Miss Foote may be deemed incidental to that. If that were to be the interpretation determined by the court, then it is arguable that the term is a warranty and any breach of it can be remedied by an award of damages.

3 The second question is whether Miss Foote has in fact breached the term of the contract. The term states that 'singing except as part of The Moves' is prohibited. If there has been no breach, Virgo Plus Ltd is not entitled to any remedy at all. Miss Foote maintains that she performed three stand-up comedy numbers which included singing a few lines. On the face of it, it does appear that Miss Foote is in breach as she concedes she sang a few lines. It would appear however that perhaps the term is construed an absolute one, given Virgo Plus Ltd's response. This point needs clarifying, as it would seem to be rather unreasonable in its import when applied to the circumstances of this particular case. If the contract intended to prevent singing, performing or entertaining, then on the face of it a breach has occurred. However, it is not the intention but the stated terms which the court will have regard to, and the term in the contract states clearly 'singing'

without The Moves would constitute a breach. A possible argument that could be raised in Miss Foote's favour is that the term as to singing is not certain and clear.

It is my opinion that, based on the papers before me, Miss Foote is not in breach of this term. However, I would like those instructing me to obtain an additional statement from Miss Foote as to any supplementary evidence or oral statements that could help to clarify the terms as stated, and for those additional statements to be forwarded to me as soon as possible. It could be the case that after analysing the performance contract and other evidence, I could take a different view.

4 Term two

The question of definition is again important before being able to venture an opinion as to breach. It seems clear enough that the term is a condition, but could only seem to be a term which could apply in respect of Miss Foote's performances with the group. Clause two seems to be an integral part of clause one. How reasonable is it for Virgo Plus Ltd to dictate Miss Foote's form of dressing when she is not performing under contract with them? The question of reasonableness will be explored fully on receipt of the copy of the contract. It could be argued that the term stands or falls with clause one. Naturally, I can only come to a firm view about this clause once I have seen a copy of the whole contract. As it is, I am unsure whether this clause goes on to restrict the wearing of gowns by Miss Foote as a member of the group, and while performing in that capacity, or generally.

5 Finally, it is my preliminary opinion that subject to the further information requested, on the face of it breaches of contract may or may not have occurred and Virgo Plus Ltd may or may not be entitled to repudiate. Much depends on what the full extent of the text of the contract is, and I wait eagerly to receive same from instructing solicitors.

25 October 1995

B A Barrister
7 Kings Court
Chancery Lane
London W11

5　　Exemption clauses

If a party seeks to rely on a clause in a contract which purports to exclude (or merely to financially limit) the party's liability for breach of contract, misrepresentation or negligence then that party must show that the clause is a valid part of the contract and that it covers the contingent liability which is sought to be excluded. Even if the party is able to show that the clause has been incorporated in the contract, and that on the clause's true construction it covers the breach which has occurred, they may still find that the clause is invalid or inoperative.

Incorporation

A person who signs a document, purporting to have contractual effect which contains an exclusion clause, is bound by its terms. It does not matter whether that person has read the terms or not, they are still bound. In *L'Estrange v Graucob* (1934), the female owner of a café purchased an automatic cigarette vending machine. She signed the agreement without reading or understanding the small print and it was held that she was bound by a clause excluding liability in damages for defects in the machine. However, where a signature is obtained using a misrepresentation as to its effect or fraud, the full force of the rule is then mitigated. In *Curtis v Chemical Cleaning and Dyeing Co Ltd* (1951), the plaintiff took a dress to be cleaned. She was induced to sign a document which, she was told, merely excluded the cleaner's liability for damage to sequins. In fact, the document excluded liability for any damage to any property deposited for cleaning. The dress was returned stained in this case and the Court of Appeal held that the defendants were not protected by the clause because it extended further than their representation.

Notice

If the exemption clause is not signed but is set out or referred to in a document which is merely delivered by one party to the other, then sufficient and reasonable notice of the existence of the exclusion clause must be given. Whether such notice has been given to the party adversely affected by the clause will depend on a number of factors.

Nature of the document

An exemption clause is only validly incorporated into a contract if the document containing the clause is a contractual one. Is the document one in which the reasonable person would expect to find contractual terms? Is the document intended to have contractual force? These questions must be affirmatively answered to enable valid incorporation of the exclusion clause into the contract. An illustration of such questions is the case of *Chapelton v Barry UDC* (1940) where a deckchair ticket was only a receipt to prove payment rather than something on which one would expect to find contractual terms. It was held that the defendants would not be protected by an exemption clause printed on the ticket. The reason was that the ticket did not purport to set out the conditions on which the plaintiff had hired the chair, but only to show for how long he had hired it and that he had paid the fee.

Degree of notice

The customer is bound by the exempting conditions if he knows that the ticket is issued subject to it. However, in practice this is difficult to show and it is now clearly the law that 'the party relying on the exemption clause need not show that he actually brought it to the notice of the other party, but only that he did what was reasonably sufficient to give him notice of it' (*Parker v South Eastern Rail Co* (1877)).

Adequacy of notice

What constitutes reasonable notice is a question of fact depending on the circumstances of the case. The individual deficiencies of a particular plaintiff or defendant will not have an overriding effect. In *Thompson v LMS Railway Co* (1930), an illiterate railway passenger was held to be bound by a clause since enough or certainly sufficient notice would have been given to a literate traveller.

Novel or unusual clauses

Further, the more unusual or serious a particular exemption or exclusion clause is, the higher the degree of notice which may be required to validly incorporate it. In *Thornton v Shoe Lane Parking Ltd*, a car-park ticket referred to a condition purporting to exclude liability for personal injury. It was held that adequate notice was not given to the driver, even though more common terms such as excluding or limiting liability for damage to the vehicle or other property may have been able to be validly incorporated by such words. However, in this instance, Lord Denning was driven to say that the exempting condition:

> is so wide and so destructive of rights that the court should not rule any man bound by it unless it is drawn to his attention in the most explicit way. It is a instance of what I had in

mind in *Spurling v Bradshaw*. In order to give sufficient notice, it would need to be printed in red ink, with a red hand pointing to it, or something equally startling.

Time of notice

The existence of the exclusion clause must be brought to the notice of the other party before or at the time the contract is formed. Notice given after the contract has been entered into is not able to incorporate the subsequent exclusion clauses into the contract without separate consideration. In *Olley v Marlborough Court* (1949), notice given after the contract was formed was told to be ineffective. In that case, the plaintiff arrived at a hotel and paid for a room in the reception. It was decided that a notice in the bedroom containing an exclusion clause was not incorporated; since the contract was formed at reception, the notice of the clause came too late to affect the plaintiff's rights.

While strictly speaking notice of exclusion clauses should always happen before the contract is formed, often the courts do not worry about split seconds so that as long as the notice of the exclusion clause is reasonably contemporaneous with the formation of the contract then generally there is not a problem. The theory is that for instance you buy a ticket and the contract is formed when the ticket is handed over. However, in most cases if the customer then saw clauses on the ticket with which he didn't agree and decided that he no longer wanted to contract then the customer would still be able to return the ticket and get his money back. The courts, however, do apply the strict rule with some vigour. In *Thornton v Shoe Lane Parking* (1971), Lord Denning MR declared conditions on a ticket issued by an automatic car park barrier came too late, the contract had been concluded a moment before when the plaintiff placed his vehicle on the spot which activated the barrier. Lord Denning concluded that the customer 'may protest to the machine, even swear at it, but it will remain unmoved – he is committed beyond recall'.

Previous dealing

Where the contracting parties have built up a course of dealing on the same terms, the fact that on a particular occasion there has been insufficient notice of the usual terms will not necessarily prevent the incorporation of the terms (*Spurling v Bradshaw* (1956)). If the transactions between the parties were separately negotiated or if they were intermittent then the courts will reject the proposition that there has been sufficient notice of the terms to incorporate them into a particular contract, the course of conduct must be consistent (*McCutcheon v David Mac Brayne Ltd* (1964)).

However, once it is shown that there is or has been a consistent course of dealings, then mere knowledge of the existence of a clause will be sufficient to bind that party by the previous course of dealing (*Hardwick Game Ltd v Suffolk Ag Producer's Association* (1969)). In contrast to dealings between businesses, a considerable number of previous transactions is required to show a course of dealings between a consumer and a business. This contrast can clearly be shown by comparing the cases of *Hollier v Rambler Motors Ltd* (1972) and *British Crane Hire Corp Ltd v Ipswich Plant Hire Ltd* (1975).

Construction

After it has been established that a clause is validly incorporated into the contract, the whole contract must be scrutinised and construed to see whether the clause covers the particular breach that has occurred. The starting point for such construction is the guiding principle that liability can only be excluded by clear words.

Contra proferentem rule

Exemption clauses are strictly construed against parties who rely on them. However, although the *contra proferentem* rule applies to all exemption clauses the courts do not apply it as strictly to clauses which merely limit liability as they do to those which attempt to exclude it totally. The reason for the courts' stance was explained by Lord Fraser in the *Ailsa Craig* (1983) case:

> the reason for imposing such standards on [exclusion and indemnity] clauses is the inherent improbability that the other party to a contract including such a clause intended to release the proferens from a liability that would otherwise fall upon him. But there is not such a high degree of improbability that we would agree to a limitation of the liability of the proferens. If the words of the exemption clause are ambiguous then they will be construed as narrowly as possible against the party attempting to rely on the clause.

Hence in *Houghton v Trafalgar Insurance Co* (1954), a policy of car insurance excluded the insurer's liability where an excessive 'load' was being carried. It was held that the clause did not extend to the situation where a five-seater car was carrying six passengers. In this instance the word 'load' was narrowly defined as referring to property/goods, not people.

Negligence

While the Unfair Contracts Act 1977 largely governs exclusion clauses that seek to exempt liability for negligence it is certain that even where the ability to exclude liability for negligence still exists, words must be very plain. The central question is always whether the intention of one party to exclude liability for negligence has been made sufficiently clear to the other. As always an express reference to negligence is the safest although not the only way of getting to the result.

In the absence of express reference, if the words used are broad enough to cover negligence, eg if there is a 'term' exempting a party from 'all liability whatsoever' then there may be a valid exclusion clause unless there is some liability other than their negligence to which the words would apply. It is often the case, as in *White v John Warwick Co Ltd* (1953), that there are dual areas of liability for breach of both contract and negligence. In cases such as this, general words like 'nothing in this agreement shall render the owners liability for personal injury' will be construed only to cover the *proferens'* liability in contract. By contrast where a contracting party is only liable for negligence, the courts will interpret an exclusion clause in general terms can cover negligence. In *Rutter v Palmer* (1922), a customer left a car with a garage for sale in the terms that 'customers' cars are driven by our staff at customers' sole risk'. In this case it was held that the garage proprietor was protected by this clause from liability caused by the negligence of one of his staff, as this was undoubtedly the clear meaning of the clause. It is at this stage worth remembering that these are only rules of construction as apart from substantive law doctrines and thus will not be exercised to defeat the intention of the parties.

Fundamental breach

In the middle of this century the courts built up a doctrine that stated that an exclusion clause could not protect a party from a fundamental (ie serious) breach of contract. This so-called 'doctrine of fundamental breach' was rejected by the House of Lords in the 1967 *Suisse Atlantique* case. The question whether an exclusion clause would apply when there was fundamental breach, or any other breach, depends on the construction of the contract as a whole. The courts role is merely to imply such a term as is needed to give the contract that business efficacy which the parties as reasonable men must have intended it to have. However, the Court of Appeal continued to apply the doctrine of fundamental breach as if it were an independent rule of law to be imposed by the courts irrespective of the parties' intention. Hence in 1980, the House of Lords reaffirmed that the 'doctrine of fundamental breach' was a rule of construction not an independent rule of law. In *Photo Production Ltd v Securicor Transport Ltd* (1980), the plaintiffs had employed the defendants to protect their factory by a visiting patrol. An exemption clause provided that 'under no circumstances shall the (defendant) company be responsible for any injurious act or default by any employee of the company'. One night, one of the defendants' guards lit a small fire inside the factory which got out of control and destroyed the plaintiff's premises with loss amounting to £615,000. The House of Lords held that though the defendants were in breach, they were permitted to rely on the clause as it clearly covered the breach in question.

Absurd or repugnant clauses

General words which at first sight appear to cover even the most serious breach may not be construed in this sense, if to give them this effect would lead to an absurdity, or because it would defeat the main object of the contract or perhaps for some other reason. For example, the courts will not protect a bailee who having undertaken to deliver goods to one person could not rely on general words of exclusion if he deliberately delivered the goods to another person, or threw them into the sea (*Sze Hai Tong Bank Ltd v Rambler Cycle Co Ltd* (1959)). There is in essence a strong although rebuttable presumption that inserting a clause of exclusion or limitation ... the parties are not contemplating breaches of fundamental terms.

Further limitations

Conflict with other express terms

An exemption clause in a document with reference to which the parties have contracted is capable of being overridden by an oral or written express undertaking at the formation of the contract. A party is not prevented on relying on a clause merely because no reference was made to it at the time of contracting. In this respect at least a claim which seems to be inconsistent with the terms expressly agreed can be relied upon. In *Mendelssohn v Normand Ltd* (1970), an oral statement by a garage attendant that the plaintiff should leave his car unlocked was held to override an exclusion clause relating to non-liability for good stolen. The defendant garage was held not to be protected by the exclusion clauses when items were stolen from the plaintiff's car.

Privity

The courts have frequently held that a person who is not a party to a contract is not protected by an exclusion clause in that contract, even if the clause attempts to extend to that person. In the leading case *Scruttons v Midland Siliconest* (1962), it was held that 'a stranger cannot in a question with either of the contracting parties take advantage of any of the provisions of the contract, even where it is clear from the contract that there was some provision in it that was intended to be of benefit to him'.

Legislation

The main piece of legislation in this area is the Unfair Contract Terms Act 1977. Its purpose is to restrict the extent to which liability in a contract can be excluded for breach of contract and negligence. The Act does not cover liabilities that are consequent on private personal transaction except in so far as it: implies terms in sale of goods and hire-purchase contracts; implies terms in the supply of goods and services contracts, and in misrepresentation. Schedule 1 to the Act does not apply to contracts such as insurance contracts. Despite this the

Act applies primarily to what are called business liabilities which are liabilities arising from things done by a person in the course of a business or from occupation of business premises.

Negligence

No term of any contract to which s 2(1) applies can exclude or restrict for death or personal injury; and liability for other types of loss can only be excluded or restricted insofar as the term or notice satisfies the requirement of reasonableness laid down by the Act s 2(2).

Contractual liability

Where one party 'deals as consumer' or on the party's written standard terms of business, then the other party cannot exclude or restrict his liability for breach of contract except subject to the requirement of reasonableness (s 3(2)(a)). The reasonableness requirement is also extended to terms purporting to entitle the other party to render: (i) performance substantially different from that reasonably expected; or (ii) no performance at all. It is the case that a person 'deals as consumer' if he does not contract in the course of a business and the other party does so contract (s 12).

Sale of goods – hire-purchase

In any contract for the sale of goods and also for contracts for hire-purchase, the implied terms as to title cannot be excluded or restricted by a contract term. As against a consumer, liability for implied terms such as merchantable quality, fitness for purpose, sample and correspondence with description. As against a business such liability can only be excluded or restricted in so far as such clause is reasonable (s 6). The reasonableness criteria applies to all liability arising under any contract of sale or hire-purchase.

Affirmation and breach

Section 9(1) holds that an exclusion clause which is required to be incorporated survives the termination of the contract either by breach or by a party electing to treat it as repudiated. In the context of breach of contract, when one speaks of termination what is meant is no more than that the innocent party or in some cases, both parties are excused from further performance. Section 9(2) makes it clear that a party who, after breach, affirms the contract, may recover damages despite an exclusion which does not satisfy the requirements of reasonableness.

Reasonableness

In order to satisfy the requirement of reasonableness, a contract term must be a fair and reasonable one to be included having regard to the circumstances which were or ought reasonably to have been known to or in the contemplation of the parties when the contract was made s 11(4). Where the contractual term purports to restrict liability to a specified sum of money. The court must have regard to the resources which the defendant could expect to have to meet the liability and how far it was open to him to cover himself by insurance: s 11(4). The onus is on the party relying on the term to establish that it satisfies the requirement of reasonableness s 11(5).

The factual analysis: opinion writing

The following case scenario will look at exemption clauses and some ancillary issues relating to these type of clauses.

CASE SCENARIO

Counsel is instructed by Dobb and Co on behalf of Mr Winston Skins, a building contractor specialising in loft conversions. Mr Skin hired some scaffolding and scaffolders from Mr Noneck. While installing the scaffolding, the scaffolders belonging to Mr Noneck broke all the windows at the back of Mr Raven's premises. There is a clause in Mr Skins' hire contract exempting all liabilities for negligence. Counsel is instructed to advise Mr Skins.

Extract of hire agreement

Noneck Inc Ltd shall be exempt for any liability for loss or damage howsoever caused to customers' premises and if, not withstanding the foregoing, any liability for damage to customers' property should arise, that liability shall be limited to a total of £250.

Statement by Winston Skins, 7 Rockingham Close, Bimshire

I am the Managing Director of Skins Loft Co Ltd. We always hire our scaffolding and scaffolders from Noneck Inc. We have been doing so for the past two years. The service is generally good; the men are prompt and careful.

In August 1994, I got a contract for a very large loft conversion. The scaffold needed to be erected at the back of the house. This was a tricky job, because there were lots of windows at the back of the house, also an all-glass conservatory. I rang Neville and asked if he had a crew available.

Neville Noneck said he had a good crew to do the job, and we agreed our usual terms. I collected the invoice as usual, after the telephone call.

The crew arrived but it seemed that one of their chaps, Joe Bash, was new to the job. He kept dropping things. I went off to another site and when I returned at tea time the whole place was in a mess. Glass was everywhere. All the back windows were shattered and the glass conservatory was virtually demolished. Mr Raven, the house owner, came home, saw the state of things and went off his head, threatening to sue me if things were not back in order by the end of the week.

I rang Neville, told him of the situation and he said I should look at the back of my hire agreement. He said it had a clause which protected his company and he was only responsible for £250 worth of damage if at all, the rest was down to me. Mr Raven has presented me with an estimate for the windows of £1,500 and for the conservatory for £1,800. I think Noneck should pay the total cost. It was not my fault. The workmen, especially Joe Bash, belonged to him.

The practical approach

Legal and factual issues

- Has the clause been incorporated into the contract between Neville Noneck and Winston Skins?

- If it has been incorporated whether on its true construction it is effective in excluding or limiting Noneck Inc's liability for damages.

- Whether the clause is affected by the Unfair Contract Terms Act 1977, the effect of ss 2, 12, and 22.

- The significance of notice of the existence of the clause to Winston Skins.

- The relevance of the 10 years course of dealings between the parties.

- Liability of Joe Bash.

- Liability of Noneck Inc.

- Course of dealings.

- An analysis of the exemption/exclusion clause.

Dramatis personae

- Winston Skins – putative first defendant – in an action brought by Mr Raven;

- Noneck Inc – second defendant in action brought by Mr Raven; third party – joined by Winston Skins if not defendant;

- Mr Raven – putative plaintiff in an action against Winston Skins;

- Joe Bash – depends on 'capacity': employee or independent contractor.

Gaps in instructions: to be requested

- Full copy of contract between Neville Noneck and Winston Skins;

- Further statement from Winston Skins – detailing the nature of the contractual relationship between the parties over the period.

THE OPINION

---

1 I am asked to advise Mr Winston Skins as to whether he could be held liable or the damage done to Mr Raven's property by workmen hired from Noneck Inc, and also whether the clause on the back of the hire contract will protect Noneck Inc, in excluding or limiting any claim he might wish to make against the company.

My initial view is that on the face of it both Joe Bash and Noneck Inc are liable for the damage caused by Joe Bash's negligence. In order to determine the effect of the contractual liability between the parties, and to assess whether and how far the exemption clause would protect Noneck Inc, it is necessary to examine the clause itself and its potential effect.

2 Skins Ltd contracted with Noneck Inc, a scaffolding company, to erect a scaffold on the site of a large job. Joe Bash, an employee of Noneck Inc, is negligent, causing scaffolding to fall, smashing glass in the windows and a large part of a glass conservatory. Mr Skins has been presented with an invoice of £3,300 by his client Mr Raven. Mr Skins presents this to Mr Noneck who denies responsibility, or in the event of accepting liability, says it is limited to £250; he relies on an exemption clause printed on the back of the hire agreement.

Whether Mr Noneck will be able to limit his liability as he claims depends on whether the clause has been incorporated into the contract made between the parties, whether on construction the clause which purports to limit or exclude liability for damage is effective.

3 Course of dealings

It appears that the contract between Mr Skins and Noneck Inc was made over the telephone and at the time there was no notification of the existence of the exemption clause to Mr Skins. This notice it seems came later, after the contract was made and the damage to the premises done. It is my view that since the contract preceded the clause, then the clause may not be held to be effective in exempting Noneck Inc. I am concerned however that there has been a consistent course of dealings between the parties over a fairly long period of time. If, as I suspect, the parties have built up a course of dealing on the same terms, then the fact that on this particular occasion there has been insufficient notice of the usual terms, will not necessarily prevent the incorporation of the terms into the contract.

57

I would be grateful for a further fuller statement from Mr Skins detailing the previous course of dealings between the parties before I am able to give a firm opinion of the issue of Mr Skins' knowledge of the clause.

If the clause is held not to be incorporated based on the previous consistent course of dealings, then the liability which Noneck purports to exclude or limit is not protected. However if the course of dealings shows that Mr Skins had notice of the clause and it is therefore properly incorporated, I must then consider the construction of the clause.

4 The exemption clause

Unfortunately, I only have an extract of the contract before me and would be grateful of those instructing me could forward to me a copy of the hire agreement in its entirety. My view of the clause, as it stands, may be subject to change once I am in receipt of the complete document. It would seem however that the wording of the clause claims to do two things: (i) exclude liability; (ii) limit liability to £250.00.

The courts generally tend to take a very strict approach in interpreting exclusion clauses, this approach has however been modified as a result of statute. The clause in Noneck Inc's hire agreement seeks to limit liability for negligence; the question is whether the words are plain and whether the intention of Mr Noneck to exclude liability for negligence has been made sufficiently clear to Mr Skins. On the face of it, the phrase is the clause 'loss or damage howsoever caused' does seem to be wide enough to include negligence, although there is no express reference to negligence.

I am not able to give my firm view as to the approach the court is likely to take in this case, should the matter proceed to litigation, but I am able to say that should there be any absurd or repugnant clauses or any evidence which shows a conflict with the clause then the court is likely to construe the clause against Noneck Inc, who are seeking to rely on it.

5 Privity – Joe Bash

It seems clear that Joe Bash who is not a party to the contract is not protected by the exclusion clause in the contract, even though the clause may attempt to extend to him. The reality of the situation is however, even if Mr Skins were to consider action against Mr Noneck's employee, the question of enforcing judgment against him may be a difficulty.

6 Reasonableness

If the matter does proceed to litigation, Mr Noneck will have to satisfy the court that the clause was a reasonable and fair one to have been included, having regard to the circumstances which were or ought reasonably to have been known, or in the contemplation of the parties when the contract was made; the court will also look at Noneck Inc's possibility to insure and also what resources the company has.

7   Finally as it stands, it seems that *prima facie* Mr Noneck may have an effective exemption clause; however this is a preliminary view that I have taken and I await the further information requested so I can take a more firm view.

16 September 1995

B A Barrister
7 Kings Court
Chancery Lane
London W11

6   Misrepresentation

False statement of fact

A statement of material fact during the negotiations made by one party to the other, which, while not being a term of the contract, induces the other party to enter the contract is a representation. Where such a statement is false you have a misrepresentation which at law is actionable. The test that the court will use to determine this is 'whether on the totality of the evidence the parties intended or must be taken to have intended that the representation was to form part of the basis of the contractual relation between them' (Ormrod LJ: *Esso Petrol Co Ltd v Mardon* (1976)).

False statement of fact: future conduct or intention

An actionable misrepresentation is a false statement of some specific existing fact or past event. A statement of intention is capable of being a statement of existing fact because as Bowen LJ remarked in *Edgington v Fitzmaurice* (1885) 'The state of a man's mind is as much a fact as the state of his digestion.' In that case company directors raised capital from the public by stating that the money would be used to expand the business. In reality the main purpose in raising money by the issue of the debenture was to pay off debts. The Court of Appeal held this representation to be a fraudulent misrepresentation of fact. In general, however the rule remains that a statement as to what one will do in the future which is false is not misrepresentation unless it is a wilful lie

False statement of fact: belief or opinion

If the opinion is not honestly held there will be an actionable misrepresentation of fact. Indeed if the representor possesses special knowledge or skill in relation to the subject-matter or is in a stronger position to know the truth, then a statement expressed as an opinion may be held to be an implied misrepresentation of fact (*Smith v Land and House Property Corporation* (1884)). Where by contrast the representor has no special knowledge, and the representee is in an equal position to the representor to verify the representation then, and the representation is honestly made the courts will not hold a representation which turns out to be false to be an actionable misrepresentation. A good example of such a case is *Bisset v Wilkinson* (1927), where the owner of a farm estimated to a prospective buyer that he thought it could support 2,000 sheep. In this case the farm had never been used previously to raise sheep and the statement was held to be of opinion rather than a statement of fact.

False statement of fact: silence or non-disclosure

Non-disclosure that leads to a statement being put forward which is not the whole truth may be a misrepresentation. Where a credit reference is required and a person neglects to disclose the fact within his knowledge that a man is a bankrupt choosing instead to say that he is honest and trustworthy, then that person may be legally regarded as having made a misrepresentation (*Tapp v Lee* (1803)). There are also circumstances where a statement is true when it is made but has become false by the time it is acted upon. In such circumstances, again the representor may be regarded to have made a misrepresentation.

A doctor ran a successful one-man medical practice and stated truthfully the value to a potential purchaser. The doctor then fell ill, so that by the time the contract was signed four months later, the receipts and the goodwill had fallen in value to almost nothing. In such a circumstance, it was held that the failure of the doctor to disclose the change of circumstances in regard to his initial representation to the purchaser became a misrepresentation. Also, wherever there is a fiduciary duty between the parties, for example in the relationships between: a doctor and a patient; a solicitor and a client; or a parent and a child, a duty of disclosure exists.

The law is unsurprisingly similar in a contract of the utmost good faith (*uberrimae fidei*), there is a duty to disclose all material facts as one party is in a strong position to know the truth. The archetypal case is that of insurance contracts, where it is clear that the insured are under a duty to disclose every circumstance which the insurers would need to set the premium or decide to take the risk. Other examples are contracts of partnership and suretyship. However, where such duties to disclose do not occur it remains a matter of good sense and law that to remain silent cannot be a representation of fact and hence not a misrepresentation in law.

False statement of fact: law

Statements as to the content of private Acts of Parliament or foreign law are held to be statements of fact, capable if false of giving rise to an action alleging misrepresentation. In contrast, false statement as to what indigenous English law is cannot be the basis for a claim of actionable misrepresentation unless they involve an implicit misstatement of fact. In *Solle v Butcher* (1950), where a landlord described his extensively redecorated and refurbished flat as 'new', this was held to be a statement of fact. This was so even when the landlord had mistakenly thought that his renovations had created a 'new' entity under the Landlord and Tenant legislation of the time and was thus free of prior Rent Act controls.

Inducement

Where a false statement has been made, and the other party despite being made aware of its nature, forms their own judgment as to the matter there is no actionable misrepresentation as the false statement when the contract is formed cannot have been relied upon. To be actionable in contract a misrepresentation must both be addressed to the other party and it must have materially induced the contract (although it need not have materially induced the whole contract exclusively). If it can be shown that the maker of a statement knows that the statement will be passed on to the plaintiff then the maker of the statement will be liable in misrepresentation. The question of what is a material objection is not viewed objectively. The initial burden of proof in such matters is on the representee to show that the statement was made and that it was capable of inducing the contract. The burden of proof then passes to the maker of the statement to show that the representee would have entered into the contract anyway, even if the misrepresentation had not been made.

Types of misrepresentation

Fraudulent

It is clear that fraudulent misrepresentation has dishonesty and deceit at its core, however there need not be an intention to cheat or to injure the person to whom the statement was made, the motive of the person is immaterial. Fraud is proved (according to Lord Herschell in the leading case of *Derry v Peek* (1889)) 'when it is shown that a false representation has been made (i) knowingly, or (ii) without belief in its truth, or (iii) recklessly, careless as to whether it be true or false.' However, Lord Herschell went on to say that to 'prevent a false statement being fraudulent, there must I think, always be an honest belief in its truth.' Hence in *Akerhielm v de Mare* (1959) where a company's prospectus stated *inter alia* that 'about a third of the capital has already been subscribed in Denmark' and this statement was false, the fact that the directors of the company believed the statement to be true at the issue of the prospectus was held by the Privy Council not to make the misrepresentation fraudulent. Where a party has been misled by a fraudulent misrepresentation they have three main remedies: affirm the contract and claim damages for the tort of deceit; rescind the contract and claim damages; or plead the fraud as a defence to any action against him for breach of contract.

Negligent misstatement under common law

A misrepresentation is negligence if it is made carelessly and in breach of a duty owed by the maker of the statement to the party who acts upon the representation to take reasonable care to ensure that the statement is accurate. In 1963, the House of Lords stated that in certain circumstances damages may be recoverable in tort for negligent misstatement leading to financial loss (*Hedley Byrne v Heller* (1963)). This dicta was clarified by the Court of Appeal in *Esso v Mardon* where it was held that where a party with special knowledge and expertise concerning the subject knowledge of pre-contract negotiation makes a forecast on that knowledge and expertise with the intention of inducing the other party to enter into the contract, and in reliance on the forecast the other party did enter into the contract, their forecast could be construed as a warranty that it was reliable, ie that it had been made with reasonable care and skill. Where the forecast was made negligently as happened in the case then the defendant would be liable for negligent misrepresentation. The crucial factor is the existence of a 'special relationship' between the parties. Such a relationship will generally occur only where the maker of the statement not only possesses relevant knowledge and skill on the contract's subject matter but can also reasonably foresee that the other party will rely on the statement.

Negligent misstatement under statute

Section 2(1) of the 1967 Misrepresentation Act holds that 'Where a person has entered into a contract after a misrepresentation has been made to him by another party thereto and as a result thereof he has suffered loss, then if the person making the representation would be liable to damages in respect thereof had the misrepresentation been fraudulently made, that person shall be so liable notwithstanding that the misrepresentation was not made fraudulently, unless he proves that he had reasonable ground to believe and did believe up to the time the contract was made that the facts represented were true.' It provided for the first time a statutory remedy for negligent and non-fraudulent misrepresentation. The creation of such a remedy has overshadowed the common law rule because the statute does not require there to be a special relationship giving rise to a duty of care between the parties and it places the burden of proof on the maker of the statement to show that they are not liable for the loss suffered by the representee. The maker of the statement is liable 'unless he proves that he had reasonable ground to believe and did in fact believe that the facts represented were true.'

Innocent misstatement

Before 1963 all non-fraudulent misrepresentations were thought to be innocent misstatements. Following *Hedley Byrne* and s 2(1) innocent misrepresentations are regarded to refer to statements made by a person who has reasonable grounds for believing in its truth. The only effect that the Misrepresentation Act has had is that s 2(2) provides that in some such circumstances the court retains an equitable jurisdiction to award damages in lieu of rescission for innocent misrepresentation. In detail the section provides: 'Where a person has entered into a contract after a misrepresentation has been made to him otherwise than fraudulently, and he would be entitled, by reason of the misrepresentation, to rescind the contract, then, if it is claimed, in any proceedings arising out of the contract, that the contract ought to be or has been rescinded, the court or administrator may declare the contract subsisting and award damages in lieu of rescission, if of opinion that it would be equitable to do so, having regard to the nature of the misrepresentation and the loss that would be caused by it if the contract were upheld, as well as to the loss that would be caused by it if the contract was upheld, as well as to the loss that rescission would cause to the other party.'

Remedies

Rescission

The general rule is that rescission is available whether the misrepresentation is innocent, negligent or fraudulent. The misrepresentation makes the contract voidable at the option of the representee, ie the representee can choose whether he wishes to set aside the contract. The importance of misrepresentation making a contract voidable can easily be illustrated. If an innocent third party obtains property that is the subject of a previous void contract then that property can be recovered from that third party. However, if such a third party receives goods that were the subject of a contract which is voidable for misrepresentation but has not been voided by the representee before passing to the innocent third party then the owner will lose the right to rescind the original contract. Rescission may be carried out quite informally by simply giving notice to the other party or in some cases by any other act that clearly indicates a repudiation of liability. In *Car and Universal Finance Ltd v Caldwell* (1964) the owner of a car had been induced by fraud to sell his car to a villain who absconded and could not be traced. When the owner discovered the fraud he notified the police and the Automobile Association to gain assistance in recovering his vehicle. The Court of Appeal held that these acts were enough to rescind the contract. The result was that an innocent third party who bought the car later got no title to it. In addition to an order of rescission the court may order an indemnity against the maker of the misrepresentation. If this is done then the misrepresentor will have to make a cash payment to the misrepresentee so that the parties can be restored to their position had the contract not been made. This is a different remedy to that of damages although it will not be used where damages are in fact awarded.

Bars to rescission

Affirmation

The representee will lose his right to rescind his contract on account of a misrepresentation if he expressly or by conduct affirms the contract after discovering the truth. Such an affirmation will take effect if the injured party expressly states that they intend to continue with the contract or if they do an act from which such intention may be implied (*Long v Lloyd* (1958)). In cases of fraud or breach of fiduciary duty, lapse of time between knowledge of the misrepresentation and rescission may be evidence of affirmation. However, in the case of non-fraudulent misrepresentation there is Court of Appeal authority for the proposition that time runs from the date of the contract not the date of discovery of the misrepresentation. In the case of *Leaf v International Galleries* the plaintiff was induced to buy a picture by the innocent misrepresentation that it was by 'J Constable'. Five years on, immediately on learning that the painting was not a Constable, the plaintiff sought to rescind but it was held that his right so to do was barred by the lapse of time even though there was no evidence of affirmation. In cases other than those of innocent misrepresentation the time which can be used as evidence of affirmation runs from the time when the fraud could with reasonable diligence been discovered.

Restitution impossible

If it is impossible to restore the parties to their original positions then the injured party will lose the right to rescind. Where the misrepresentee has so changed the nature of the subject matter of the contract that he can no longer restore what he obtained under the contract it would be unjust to allow him to rescind the contract. A simple example is where a representee purchases a mine, despite an actionable misrepresentation the misrepresentee cannot rely on his right to rescind the contract if he has worked the mine out (*Clarke v Dickson* (1858)). The mere fact that the representee has received a benefit under the contract does not bar his right to rescind, if the maker of the misrepresentation has not been put to any expense in providing that benefit. In equity a representee who is able to make substantial but not precise restitution is required if the representee is able to account for any profits made and for the deterioration caused by his dealing in it. In *Erlanger v New Sombero Phosphate Co* (1878), mining case, the defendant company had bought and worked a phosphate mine without working it out. The House of Lords held that rescission could occur as equity could take account of the profits and make allowance for deterioration.

Damages

Fraudulent misrepresentation

A person who suffers loss as a result of acting in reliance on a fraudulent statement can recover damages in an action of deceit. He can generally do this whether he rescinds the contract or not. The object is to restore the person to the position that they would have been in had the representation not been made. The person can therefore claim for the loss of bargain costs. The test of remoteness in deceit is that the plaintiff may recover for all the direct loss incurred as a result of the fraudulent inducement, regardless of foreseeability (*Doyle v Olby (Ironmongers) Ltd* (1969)).

Negligent misrepresentation

The plaintiff who suffers loss due to negligent misrepresentation may elect to claim damages in tort under the common law *Hedley Byrne* principle provided the elements are established. The award under *Hedley Byrne* differs from damages in deceit because under *Hedley Byrne* the remoteness test is that of reasonable foreseeability. Alternatively the plaintiff may claim damages for misrepresentation under s 2(1) of the Act of 1967. In that case his damages will be assessed on the same basis as fraudulent misrepresentation (*Royscott Trust Ltd v Rogerson* (1992)). Where the plaintiff has entered a contract as a result of misrepresentation this will be the usual course to pursue. Furthermore where a misrepresentation is made by an agent of the contracting party, the injured party can only bring an action under s 2(1) alone against the contracting party and not the agent.

Excluding liability

Further to the usual rules limiting the effect of exclusion clauses, s 3 of the 1967 Act provides that: 'if a contract contains term which would exclude or restrict (a) any liability to which a party to a contract may be subject by reason of any misrepresentation made by him before the contract was made; or (b) any remedy available to another party to the contract by reason of such a misrepresentation, that term shall be of no effect except in so far as it satisfies the requirement of reasonableness as stated in s 11(1) of the Unfair Contract Terms Act 1977; and it is for those claiming that the term satisfies that requirement to show that it does.' The section's effect cannot be evaded by a contractual term which seems to deem that statements of fact are not representations (*Cremdean Properties v Nash* (1977)). In contrast a term which says that the agreement contains the entire terms of the contract will not be invalidated by the section. Likewise the section's effect may be evaded as demonstrated in *Overbrooke Estates Ltd v Glencombe Properties Ltd* (1974), where there was a term that stated that the auctioneer had no authority to make any representations.

CASE SCENARIO

Counsel is instructed to advise Greta Richards as to what options are open to her in this matter. She purchased a violin from John Prince on the basis that it was a genuine Stradivarius and paid £25,000. It seems based on what John Prince said Greta Richards was induced to purchase the violin. It now seems that having taken it to experts at Sorbeys Miss Richards has been sold a fake. She wants her £25,000 back and also wants to be compensated after not being able to play the Stradivarius at a famous black tie gala. She had to hire an alternative, genuine Stradivarius for £1,500.

Counsel will find herewith:

(i) a statement by Miss Richards;

(ii) extract of a report from Mr Twee at Sorbeys, an expert in Stradivarius violins.

Counsel is asked to help generally.

Statement by Miss Greta Richards

I am a concert violinist. I have played at many famous functions and recently have promised to treat myself by buying a Stradivarius as a 40th birthday present. On the 24 June 1994, I went walking down Covent Garden in the Mall, and I passed a new shop. It was called J Prince Inc Fine Instruments. I went in to browse as I had seen an advert in the *Evening Post* the day before that had advertised a Stradivarius. They had said it was in immaculate condition and was 100 years old. A gentleman came out to help me. He asked whether I was looking for anything in particular. I said I was on my way to the Haymarket to look at Stradivarius violins. He then said it was a coincidence, because he had just the thing for me. He went into his stock cupboard and brought out a violin wrapped in muslin embossed with Stradivarius insignia on the rear side. It looked beautiful and I was positive that it was genuine. Mr Prince then said he had bought the violin last week from an old artiste from Vienna who had told him that the violin was genuine and gave a beautiful sound when it was played and was 100 years old. Mr Prince said he didn't know much about violins as he sold mostly wind instruments but he felt after doing some research that this was a Stradivarius.

After hearing what he had to say and examining the violin myself I felt I couldn't leave it. The price was just right. I knew that I had been quoted much more by shops in the Haymarket and therefore, based on what he said, I bought the violin. It cost £25,000. I took it to a friend, Josh Bevan, the next week to show it off and he immediately told me that I had been conned. He told me that he was something of a Stradivarius expert and it was patently obvious that this violin was not even a good imitation of a Stradivarius. The monogram on the rear was not authentic.

Josh and I went back to John Prince the next day and demanded our money back. Mr Prince refused and said he had sold the violin in good faith believing it to be a Stradivarius and that was an end to the matter. I was due to play at Sea Winds Grand Gala the following week and had advertised that I would be playing a Stradivarius violin. I had to hire one for the evening and that cost me £1,500.

Extract from Mr Twee, expert in musical instruments

I have been an examiner of violins for the past 15 years. I have seen and examined many violins including a number of Stradivarius. The violin which Miss Richards asked me to examine is not a Stradivarius. In my view its real value is no more than £500.

The practical approach

In order to advise the client, clearly counsel should isolate the various issues relating to the problem. These issues must be broken down and identified clearly. The analysis must be practical and relate to the facts presented. It is important to look at what has happened and then using the legal framework address the legal issues presented.

Legal/factual issues

- Did Greta Richards rely on the representations made by John Prince as to the genuineness of the article?

- Did this representation induce her to buy the violin?

- Were the representations fraudulent, negligent or innocent?

- Could Mr Prince argue that the advertisement in the *Evening Post* was a mere trade puff?

- What damages are open to Miss Richards?

Dramatis personae

- Miss Richards – putative plaintiff;

- Mr Prince – putative defendant;

- Mr Adam Twee – expert witness.

Gaps in instructions: to be requested

- Copy of the full report from Mr Hilary Twee;
- Statement from Mr Josh Bevan.

OPINION

Greta Richards v John Prince

1   I am asked to advise Greta Richards as to what course of action she can take in recovering £25,000 paid for a violin and also hire fees that she had to pay as a result in order to hire a substitute violin for the evening to play at a very important gala event. It seems that Miss Richards bought the violin from Mr Prince believing that she was buying a Stradivarius.

2   The first issue to resolve is whether what was said to Greta Richards by John Prince amounts to an action of a misrepresentation. Were the statements, both oral and in writing, ie the advert, made by John Prince statements of fact which induced Greta Richards to enter the contracts, ie to buy the violin. There does not seem to be any difficulty as far as I am concerned here. John Prince categorically stated both in the advert and when Greta Richards visited the shop that he had a Stradivarius violin for sale. It is my view that he can't then be heard to say that he was making a statement of his opinion. I am also satisfied that based on what Greta Richards had been told, she bought the violin. It is clear in my view that she would not simply have gone to the shop and bought the violin had she not been persuaded of its unique value as a Stradivarius.

3   Initially I am tempted to allege fraudulent misrepresentation against John Prince. However, I must weigh the advantages against the disadvantages of such an allegation. The burden of proof of fraud would rest clearly on Miss Richards, and the standard of proof is high. I think Miss Richards would be better advised to pursue her claim against John Prince under s 2(1) of the Misrepresentation Act of 1967. The advantage of doing so is that the burden of proof would be shifted on to Mr Prince and it would be for him to show that he had reasonable grounds for believing the representations to be true. I suspect he will probably attempt to rely on the statement of the Viennese artist who he said sold it to him. However, I doubt whether he will be able to convince the court that as a seller of instruments he was unable to differentiate between an ordinary violin and a Stradivarius.

4   If Miss Richards' claim were to be pursued under s 2(2) of the Misrepresentation Act 1967, this would limit any damages recoverable as damages are awarded under s 2(2) at the court's discretion and Miss Richards may be unable to recover for the hire of the alternative violin.

Instructing solicitors will see that I have pleaded s 2(1) as this leaves the burden of proof on Mr Prince and allows Miss Richards to obtain both damages and rescission for negligent misrepresentation.

5 It is my opinion that Miss Richards has a reasonably good chance of success in establishing misrepresentation under s 2(1) of the Misrepresentation Act 1967 and accordingly of rescinding the contract, thereby recovering her £25,000 and also the £1,500 for hiring the alternative violin. Instructing solicitors will find attached herewith a draft copy of a statement of claim. It is my opinion that it should be served forthwith as this may have the effect of persuading Mr Prince to negotiate and settle the matter.

B A Barrister
7 Kings Court
Chancery Lane
London W11

IN THE HIGH COURT OF JUSTICE   C1994 R No

QUEENS BENCH DIVISION

BETWEEN   Greta Richards   *Plaintiff*

                                  and

                              John Prince   *Defendant*

STATEMENT OF CLAIM

---

1   The defendant is and was at all material times the owner and Managing Director of Prince Inc, Fine Instruments.

2   In or about May 1994 the defendant advertised for sale in the Evening Post a Stradivarius violin, represented as 100 years old and with a beautiful sound, also in immaculate condition. The plaintiff in response to the said advertisement went to see the violin at the premises of the defendant, 248a Covent Garden.

3   On the 24th June 1994 at 248a Covent Garden the defendant, in order to induce the plaintiff to enter into a contract for the sale of the said violin orally represented to the plaintiff that:

   (a) it was a genuine Stradivarius violin that gave a beautiful sound when played;

   (b) that he had purchased it from an owner who was the sort of person to take good care of it; and

   (c) that it was 100 years old and in immaculate condition.

4   In reliance upon the said advertisement in the Evening Post and the defendant's oral representations the plaintiff entered into a contract with the defendant for the sale of the said violin, paid to the defendant the sum of £25,000 by banker's draft and took delivery of the violin.

5   In fact the said advertisement and oral representation were false and were made negligently in that:

   (a) the said violin was not 100 years old;

   (b) the said violin did not give a beautiful sound when played and was not in immaculate condition;

   (c) the defendant is and was at all material times the owner and Managing Director of John Prince, Fine Instruments and knew a great deal about musical instruments;

(d) the original owner was not a Viennese artist.

6   By reason of the matters aforesaid the plaintiff has suffered loss and damage.

Particulars of damage

(a) Difference in value between the violin as represented and the true value, £24,500;

(b) Cost of hiring an alternative violin, £1,500.

7   The plaintiff claims interest pursuant to s 35 of the Supreme Court Act 1981 for such sums and for such amounts as the court thinks fit.

AND the plaintiff claims:

  (i)   rescission of the said contract;

  (ii) return of the said sum, £24,500;

  (iii) further or alternatively damages;

  (iv) interest pursuant to s 35a of the Supreme Court Act.

13 June 1994

B A Barrister
7 Kings Court
Chancery Lane
London W11

7   Mistake and frustration

Mistake

Introduction

There is no such entity as a doctrine of mistake. Instead, the situations in which a contract will be nullified or capable of rescission for mistake are contained in a disparate group of cases. A mistake which renders a contract void is described as an 'operative' mistake. A mistake as to law, as opposed to a mistake of fact, will not be operative. At common law the effect of an operative mistake is generally to make the contract void *ab initio*. In such a case it does not matter how blameless the parties are or how the mistake arose. No obligations can arise under such a contract, nor can arise under such a contract, nor can title in goods pass. In equity, on the other hand, a contract affected by mistake may be voidable at the option of the party who is mistaken. Until the mistaken party chooses to avoid the contract properly will pass and obligations arise. However, the right to rescind may be lost if the subject matter of a contract affected by mistake has passed to a *bona fide* purchaser for value without notice of the circumstances of the mistake.

Mistake at common law

The general rule is that if the mind of one of the parties, or even both of the parties, at the formation of the contract, are affected by mistake, then at common law, the contract remains valid and enforceable notwithstanding the mistake (*Bell v Lever Bros* (1932)). It is only in limited circumstances that the common law validity of the contract will be effected to make the contract void. The central issue is whether in a particular case, the mistake is operative. There is operative mistake when a mistake of fact prevents the formation of any contract at all. Where it occurs, the courts will declare the agreement void: but where the mistake does not prevent the formation of agreement the contract is good and valid in the eyes of the common law. Operative mistake may occur in a number of circumstances.

Mistake as to the existence of subject matter

A contract will be void at common law where both parties are mistaken as the existence of the subject matter. The most frequent circumstance which leads to the parties consent being nullified is where the subject matter of the agreement does not exist or ceases to exist or has ceased to exist. In *Couturier v Hastie* (1856), a cargo of corn had to be sold at a port *en route* to its destination as it had begun to ferment. Unaware of this fact, both the parties had agreed a sale of the corn in London. It was held by the House of Lords that the seller was not entitled to the price of the cargo. Similarly it has also been held that a separation deed between a woman and man, who were suffering under the mistake that they were married to each other, was entirely void as it attempted to deal with a marriage that simply did not exist. Now this is (so far as sale of goods is concerned) by s 6 of the Sale of Goods Act 1979. This section provides that 'where there is a contract for the sale of specific goods, and the goods without the knowledge of the seller have perished at the time when the contract was made, the contract is void.'

Common mistake as to quality

Mistakes as to quality will only nullify the consent of the parties of the quality which the subject matter to the contract lacks, if 'it is as to the existence of some quality which makes the thing without the quality essentially different from the thing as it was believed to be' (Lord Atkin in *Bell v Lever Bros*).

The usual course of events where the subject matter if a contract lacks some quality which forms part of the contractual description of the thing, is that the contract is held to be valid and the person who gave the description in breach. Where there is an identical mistake as to the quality of the subject matter, this will not usually be operative at common law. In the *Bell v Lever Bros* case, Bell was chairman of Lever Bros, he had entered into an agreement to terminate his employment under which he was paid £30,000 compensation. After the termination and payment it was discovered that Bell could have been summarily dismissed without compensation for breach of his terms of employment. This was a case where there had been no fraud or fraudulent concealment on Bell's behalf and so the House of Lords were prepared to treat the case as a common mistake as to qualify, but held the contract valid. This case has been followed by *Leaf v International Galleries* (1950), where a painting was sold which both parties (at the time of sale) believed to have been painted by Constable, and therefore valuable. It later transpired that the painting was not a Constable and therefore worth a lot less but the contract was held valid in the absence of actionable misrepresentation or the assumption of risk in the matter by the other party. Similarly in *Harrison and Jones v Bunten and Lancaster* (1953), a contract was made for the sale of 'Sree' brand of Calcutta kapok when it was not. Nevertheless, the contract was held valid even though the impure kapok was of no use to the buyer.

Mutual mistake as to identity of subject matter

In this sort of case, the courts will consider whether a reasonable third party would take the agreement to mean what one party or the other understood it to mean. It is only when the identity of the subject matter is totally ambiguous under this objective test that the contract is void. In *Raffles v Wichelhaus* (1864), there was a contract for the sale of 125 bales of cotton 'to arrive ex Peerless from Bombay'. There were two ships named Peerless leaving Bombay at about the same time: the buyer meant one and the seller meant the other. It was held that the contract was void as it was clear that the parties had negotiated entirely at cross purposes. In an auction case, *Scriven v Hindley* (1913), Hindley's bid for a lot of consisting of tow was accepted. The defendant believed that they had bid for hemp. Their bid was right for hemp but was extravagant for tow, although the auctioneer was unaware of the true nature of the defendants' mistake. However, the catalogue an samples were misleadingly described and marked, and these factors when considered with the other circumstances meant that the reasonable person could not say whether the contract was for hemp or tow. The contract was held to be void.

Unilateral mistake

Where one party is fundamentally mistaken concerning the contract and the other party is aware of the mistake, or the circumstances are such that he may be taken to have snapped up the defendants' offer knowing there was a mistake in expressing its terms. In *Hartog v Colin and Shields* (1939), the defendants made an offer to sell to the plaintiff 30,000 Argentinian hare skins, the price being quoted in pence per pound. However, immediately before this offer the parties had negotiated in terms of prices per piece, ie in the usual trade practice. The offer was accepted before the defendants discovered that they had made a mistake in expressing their offer. Once the defendants discovered the mistake they refused to deliver the skins claiming that there was no binding contract due to mistake. The plaintiff brought an action for breach of contract to deliver the pieces. The plaintiffs were unsuccessful as the court held that the plaintiff must have realised the defendant's error which as it concerned a term of the contract rendered the contract void.

Where by contrast such a mistake is not known or deemed to be known, the acceptance will conclude a binding contract then the mistake will have no effect. In *Crowshaw v Pritchard* (1899), a builder made a mistake in calculating his offer price to do some building work and the offer was accepted. The builder then realised his mistake and wrote to the offeree explaining that in the circumstances he must withdraw the offer. After having the work carried out by another builder, the offeree had then sued for the difference between the price paid and the offer price. The builder was held to be liable as the mistake did not affect the existence of a valid contract and the builder had in essence merely sought to extricate himself form a bad bargain. A mere error of judgment as the quality or the value of contractual subject matter will not render a contract void for unilateral mistake. The defendant in *Smith v Hughes* was shown some oats.

The defendant bought them thinking that they were old oats. In reality they were new oats and the fact that the plaintiff knew of the mistake could not render the contract void.

Unilateral mistake as to nature of document

There is a general rule that a person is bound by the terms of any document which he has signed or applied his seal to even if it is the case that he did not read it, or understand its contents (*L'Estrange v Graucob* (1934)). However, an exception arises where a person signs or seals a document under a mistaken belief as to the nature of the document and the mistake was due to either (1) blindness, illiteracy, or senility of the person signing, or (2) a trick or fraudulent misrepresentation as to the nature of the document, provided that the person took all reasonable precautions and was not careless before signing. The essence of the plea of *non est factum* (this is not my deed) is that the person believes that the document he signed had one character or one effect whereas in fact its character or effect was quite different. There is a heavy burden in proof on the person who seeks to invoke the remedy because the matter generally arises where an innocent third party has relied on a signed document and is allowed to have it declared a nullity.

The restrictions on the plea of *non est factum* are demonstrated by the House of Lords case of *Saunders v Anglia Building Society* (1970) where an elderly widow wished to transfer her house to her nephew by way of gift. Her nephew and a man named Lee prepared a document assigning the property to Lee and asked her to sign. She had no hesitation in signing the document unread and without her spectacles as she had lost them. The man Lee then mortgaged the property to the Anglia and disposed of the money raised for his own use. He defaulted on the repayments and the Building Society sought possession of the house. The House of Lords held that the plaintiff fell very short of making the clear and satisfactory case which is required to have her agreement declared void by establishing a sufficient discrepancy between her intention and her act. She had been careless in not establishing that the transfer was to whom she had intended to benefit. The House of Lords refused to grant a declaration that the assignment was void due to the defence of *non est factum*.

Mistaken identity

Where there is unilateral mistake as to the identity of the other contracting party, then, despite the differences from other examples of operative mistake, the contract may be void at common law. For the contract to be void, the identity of the other party must be of crucial importance; the mistaken party must have in mind an identifiable person with whom they intend to contract; and the other party must be aware of the mistake. Where a fraudulent person conceals his true identity in order to gain possession of goods without payment, he obtains a voidable title to the goods. With any attempt by such fraudulent person to resell, s 23 of the Sale of goods Act 1979 provides that, 'When the seller of goods has a voidable title to them, but his title has not been voided at the time of sale, the buyer acquired a good title to the goods, provided he buys them in good faith and without notice of the seller's defect in title.'

Identity must be crucial

The cases regarding this particular area are very confused. Identity was held not to be crucial in *Phillips v Brooks* (1919). In this case a man named North purported to be Sir George Bullough of St James' Square (a man of great means) and wrote out a cheque in this name to purchase a ring. North then pledged the ring with innocent third parties. The deceived jeweller attempted to recover the ring from the defendants but it was held that the contract between the plaintiffs and North was not void for mistake as the plaintiffs had intended to contract with the person in the shop. The mistake that occurred concerned the customer's credit-worthiness, not his identity. The contract was, however, voidable for fraud but because the defendants had acquired the ring in good faith before the plaintiffs had attempted to set aside the contract, they had acquired good title. This decision was followed in the Court of Appeal case of *Lewis v Averay* (1973) where a student who had advertised his car for sale accepted a cheque from a man posing as Richard Greene. The cheque was proved worthless and the villain sold the car to an innocent third party, the defendant. The Court of Appeal again took the view that the contract was only voidable. Where parties are face to face, there is a presumption that a person intends to deal with the person before him, as identified by sight and hearing.

These cases contrast sharply with *Ingram v Little*, where two elderly ladies offered their car for sale to a man calling himself Mr Hutchinson from an address in Caterham. The plaintiffs checked out the name and address (as the plaintiff in *Phillips v Brooks* had done) and it was with this person they intended to deal.'Mr Hutchinson's cheque was not honoured and the car was traced again to innocent third parties who had bought it in good faith. The plaintiffs succeeded in recovery of the car or its value as it was held that the plaintiff's offer was made to the person whom the swindler pretended to be and the swindler knew this. The majority of the Court of Appeal, therefore, felt that the offer was not capable of being accepted by the swindler, therefore there was no contract and the plaintiffs were entitled to recover the vehicle or its value from the defendants (even though the defendants bought the car in good faith from the man purporting to be Hutchinson). This decision has not been recently followed. Some indication of its particular rationale can be gained from Devlin LJ's dissenting judgment where he says 'for the doing of justice the relevant question in this sort of case is not whether the contract was void or voidable, but which of two innocent parties shall suffer for the fraud of a third'.

Mistake in equity

'Mistake which renders the contract not void but voidable, that is liable to be set aside on such terms as the court sees fit, which is the kind of mistake which was dealt with by the court of equity': *Solle v Butcher per* Denning LJ. Equity will sometimes afford relief to a party who has created contractual obligation by mistake. The relief sought can take various forms:

Rescission on terms

In cases where there is a common mistake by the parties as to the facts or as to their relative and respective rights, equity may allow rescission of the contract provided that the party who is adversely affected was not at fault and subject to the claimant entering into a reformed contract with the other party containing equitable terms as ordered by the court (*Solle v Butcher* (1950), *Grist v Bailey* (1966)). In *Solle v Butcher*, a flat was extensively refurbished, altered and let. Both the landlord and tenant mistakenly believed that because of the improvement, the flat was no longer covered by the Rent Acts (as it had changed its identity). The parties thought that the flat was now free from rent control and the rent was increased from £140 to £250 per annum. When it later transpired that the flat was still covered by rent control, the tenant sought a declaration of rent at £140 and attempted to recover the excess already paid. The Court of Appeal held that although the lease was valid in law, equity demanded that it be rescinded due to the parties' mistake of fact. The landlord was therefore entitled to have the lease set aside in equity on the condition that the tenant should be granted a new lease at the full permitted rent (but not over £250). Similarly in *Grist v Bailey*, the courts refused to compel a party to sell a house for the agreed price when both parties had agreed the price under the misapprehension that it contained a statutory tenant. The house had no statutory tenant and it was clear that this mistake was fundamental. The court therefore ordered rescission subject to the condition that the defendant enter a fresh contract at a proper vacant possession price.

Rectification

In the situation where a written document does not express the actual contractual agreement between the parties, the court may order rectification of the document; it must be shown that a complete and certain agreement existed between the parties (*Joscelyne v Nissen* (1970)), that the agreement was unchanged at the time it was put into writing, and that the written document did not accurately represent what was earlier agreed (*Craddock Brothers v Hunt* (1923)).

Refusal of specific performance

A court will not usually order specific performance against a defendant who was suffering under a relevant mistake at the formation of the contract. However, those who come to equity must do so with clean hands and as the courts will refuse specific performance where the plaintiff knew of or caused the defendant's mistake (*Webster v Cecil* (1861)) just as easily as they will order specific performance against a mistaken defendant where the mistake is a result of the defendant's own carelessness (*Tamplin v James* (1880)).

Frustration

Before the case of *Taylor v Caldwell* (1863), common law held that once a party had bound themselves to a contract, no matter what, they were obliged to fulfil their obligations under it, even if they could derive no benefit from the contract. The law applied with equal vigour when a party found himself bound by a contract that was impossible to perform unless the contract had made express provision for the events. In *Taylor v Caldwell*, a music hall was hired by Taylor for four concerts but before the first one could take place the music hall burnt down. There was no fault on either party in this eventuality and the contract between them contained no clause as to the effect of fire. Both parties were excused from performance of the contract. The court denied that an implied condition about the existence of the hall should be read into the contract, since the hall no longer existed, the contract was impossible to fulfil and the parties should be relieved of their obligations.

In subsequent cases, while the doctrine of frustration has gone from strength to strength, its juristic basis has changed. In cases such as *Davis Contractors v Fareham UDC* (1956), it was held that there must be a change in the significance of the obligation that the thing undertaken would, if performed be a different thing from that contracted. It is an objective test and does not depend on repudiation by the parties. Discharge occurs automatically on the frustration. In *Joseph Constantine Steamship v Imperial Smelting Corp* (1942), Viscount Simon LC stated that the:

> doctrine of discharge from liability by frustration has been explained in various ways, sometimes by speaking of the disappearance of a foundation which the parties assumed to be at the basis of their contract, sometimes as flowing from the inference of an implied term. Whichever way it is put, the legal consequence is the same.

The situations in which a contract may become frustrated cannot all be listed. Here are some of the more frequently occurring situations.

Impossibility

A contract may, as in *Taylor v Caldwell* become entirely impossible to perform where the subject matter is destroyed. Similarly, if the subject matter (through

81

the fault of neither party) becomes unavailable, a contract may be frustrated. This was the case in *Nicholl v Ashton Eldridge* (1901), where a ship required for the performance of a contract was left stranded. By contrast in *Tsirkiroglou v Noblee Thorl* (1962), the ship was not stranded but the closure of the Suez Canal had made the contract to transport the cargo more onerous as it would have to take the route round the Cape of Good Hope. The House of Lords refused to hold the contract frustrated despite the fact that the parties had envisaged the usage of Suez; they felt that the voyage around the Cape was not fundamentally commercially different. Hence it can be safely submitted that where a particular method of performance becomes impossible the contract will only be frustrated where the method is essential to the performance of the contract and it was either expressly or impliedly stipulated in the contract itself. If further performance is rendered illegal by a change in the law, a contract will also be deemed frustrated.

Radical change

As seen in *Tsarkiraglou v Noblee Thorl*, a contract will not be frustrated where a change of circumstances renders it more onerous to perform but not radically different. In *Davis v Fareham UDC* (1956), the House of Lords refused to hold a building contract frustrated where, because of shortfalls in manpower, the work building took three times longer than had been agreed. However, in *Krell v Henry* (1903) the Court of Appeal held that where a room was let for the purpose of viewing the procession on coronation day and the coronation was cancelled that frustrated the contract. Where, by contrast in *Herne Bay Steam Boat Co v Hutton* (1903), the hire of a steamboat was for the dual purpose of viewing the King's naval review and a cruise round the harbour, the cancellation of the King's naval review alone could not frustrate the contract.

Frustration of leases

For hundreds of years the common law position was as described in *Paradine v Jane* (1648) 'when the party to his own contract creates a duty or a charge upon himself, he is bound to make it good, if he may, notwithstanding any accident by inevitable necessity, because he might have provided against it by his contract.' It was thought *inter alia* 'that the lessee is to have the advantage of casual profits, so he must run the hazard of casual loss, and not lay the whole burden of them upon his lessor; and that though the land be surrounded, or gained by the sea, or made barren by wildfire yet the lessor shall have his whole rent.' However in 1981, in *National Carriers Ltd v Panalpina (Northern) Ltd* (1981) the House of Lords decided by a majority, that a lease could be frustrated although very rarely.

Limits to frustration

The onus of proving 'frustration' lies on the party alleging it. A contract will not be discharged for frustration where one party by their conduct decides to make performance impossible (*Maritime National Fish v Ocean Trawlers Ltd* (1935)). Such action is known as self-induced frustration and the party in fault is liable for the breach of the contract. A party will also be liable for breach of contract where because of their own special knowledge, they foresaw or should have foreseen the frustrating event (*Walton Harvey Ltd v Walker and Hamofrays Ltd* (1931)). The situation appears to be different where both parties foresaw or should have foreseen the event, but made no provision to deal with it in the contract. The case of *WJ Tatem v Gamboa* (1938) provides authority for the proposition that in such a situation the contract may nevertheless be frustrated.

Legal effect of frustration

The effect of frustration on a contract is to discharge all future performance. It ends the contract unlike where in a breach of contract, the injured party may elect or not to repudiate or affirm. Prior to 1943, the situation appeared to be that where there was no total failure of consideration the loss would lie where it fell at the time of the frustrating event. There was no right to the restitution of money paid over before the frustration (*Chandler v Webster* (1904)). In 1943, the Law Reform (Frustrated Contracts) Act was introduced and its main provision s 1(2) provides that 'All sums paid or payable to any party in pursuance of the contract before the time when the parties were so discharged shall in the case of sums so paid be recoverable from him as money received by him for the use of the party by whom the sums were paid and in the case of sums so payable, cease to be payable.' In addition s 1(3) provides that 'a party who has incurred expenses in performing the contract prior to frustration may recover expenses and a party who has derived any valuable benefit from the contract as performed, must pay for it.' The only contracts to which the act does not apply are: voyage charter parties, all contracts for carriage of goods by sea, insurance contracts and contracts for the sale of specific goods which are frustrated by the goods perishing.

CASE SCENARIO

Instructing solicitors act for Dodie Bush Loft Company Ltd. On 12 June 1994 Bush Co entered into an agreement with Channer Development Co Plc. The terms of the agreement were:

'Agreed to build loft room with *en suite* bathroom at Northboro, in accordance with attached plans and specifications. Price: £13,000 all in. Work to begin on 5 July 1994 and loft to be completed including decoration by September 1994. Payments to be made in stages, £3,000 on commencement, £1,000 when the roof is on, £3,000 when the stairs are up, £2,000 when the floors are down, £3,000 when the plumbing and electrical works have been done, the balance of £1,000 to be paid one month after works have been completed.'

Bush Co began work and received the first payment as per the agreement. When the floors went down on 5 August but before Channer Development Co made the stage payment of £3,000, a government order was made requisitioning the building for use as a temporary barracks for soldiers returning from the Bedan War. The requisition order was to last for two years. Channer Development Co insist that the works must be completed for the agreed price as soon as the building is released by the government. Bush wants to terminate the contract and be compensated, maintaining that they have spent more than they have earned so far and that they would lose any projected profit as a result of the long delay should they resume work in two years.

The practical approach

This problem is designed to isolate the essential issues relating to a simple situation of frustration in contract law.

Legal and factual issues

- Has the contract been frustrated or suspended?

- What effect does the frustration have on the contract?

- Can Channer Development force Dodie Bush Loft Co Ltd to complete the contract as per the terms of the agreement dated 12 June 1994?
- Can Dodie Bush be released of their contractual obligations?

Dramatis personae

- Dodie Bush Loft Co Ltd – plaintiff;
- Channer Development Co – defendant.

Gaps in instructions: to be requested

- Full copy of the contract between the parties;
- Copy of the requisition order.

OPINION

Dodie Bush v Channer Development Co Plc

1   I am asked to advise Dodie Bush Loft Co Ltd as to whether they can escape the remaining contractual obligations to Channer Development Co Plc. In June 1994 Dodie Bush and Channer Development agreed that Dodie Bush would build a loft room and an *en suite* bathroom to a work payments schedule. Three weeks after work began the government requisitioned the building in order to accommodate soldiers returning from the Bedan War. The use of the building was requisitioned for two years. Dodie Bush Co wants to terminate the contract and maintains that they have lost on the job and will make no profit. Channer Development insist that after the requisition ceases the contract is to recommence at the agreed price.

2   The main question is whether the building contract between Dodie Bush Co and Channer Development Co Plc has reached such a situation that it can be termed frustrated. The cases tend to be clear that requisition of property which was subject to contract by the government can lead to frustration. However, requisition in itself does not lead to frustration and the other elements of frustration must be examined to determine whether an agreement between Dodie Bush Co and Channer Development Co Plc has in fact been frustrated. The crux of the matter is the effect of frustration on the contractual obligations of the parties. The effect of the requisition order is to delay the carrying out of the contract by Bush. Will the delay make the original contractual obligations very different from the ultimate performance? In my opinion the undue delay before Bush can complete the contract is not what the parties reasonably contemplated at the inception of the contract. In my view the contract is therefore frustrated. Neither party anticipated a requisition order or the delay that such an event would cause. Bush will not be able to honour the work schedule. The prices of building materials would have increased, thus making the commission of the contract unprofitable and perhaps even a liability for Bush.

3   Channer Development Co may argue that because the requisition is for a fixed period, Bush should be required to carry out the contracts as per the original agreement because the contract has been suspended and not frustrated. Therefore the works should be able to be carried out under a similar schedule as soon as a requisition order has been lifted. They may also argue that the effect of the delay does not make the agreement that different to the

original contract as Bush must still build a loft to the same specifications and with the same materials. However, my view is that indeed the contract has changed in a very fundamental way as the cost element would be significantly different for Bush as he would be expected to offset what would now be a much more expensive and onerous agreement. Channer Development on the other hand will be the recipients of a bonus as a result of the requisition order. If the court is with me and agrees that the contract has been frustrated, Channer Development will not be able to insist on Bush completing the contract on the same terms. The contract should now be regarded as terminated as to future performance.

4   Any payments made or expenses incurred by the parties before frustration will be covered by the Law Reform (Frustrated Contracts) Act 1943. Section 1(2) of the Act will allow Bush to keep the first three payment of £9,000 as all this money was used, I am assuming, in connection with the first three stages of the building works. It is my view that Bush will be able to recover the stage payment of £3,000 after the floors went down under s 1(3), as it is easy to show that this is clearly a valuable benefit on Channer Development. It is my opinion that Channer Development will want to resist making this payment and argue that there have been no benefits offered; their perceived argument will be: to what use could they put the floors since they cannot use it for the purpose for which it was constructed and it would simply be lying there. I think this objection can be overcome quite easily by Bush showing that they incurred expenses in laying the floors and also that these floors wouldn't be laid again at the end of the frustrating event. I have not been told by instructing solicitors of any additional expenses incurred by Bush in relation to the building. Could instructing solicitors kindly inform me of these details if they are appropriate.

5   It is my opinion that Bush should attempt to renegotiate the contractual terms with Channer Development as the cost implications for litigation could be significant in relation to the amount outstanding on the contract. I have however drafted a statement of claim. Instructing solicitors will find it attached herewith. I am of the view that although the sum involved is well within the County Court limits of £50,000, the issues may be more appropriate for a High Court Judge.

B A Barrister
7 Kings Court
Chancery Lane
London W11

IN THE HIGH COURT OF JUSTICE   1994 B No

QUEENS BENCH DIVISION

BETWEEN   Bush Loft Co Ltd   *Plaintiffs*

and

Channer Development Co Plc   *Defendants*

STATEMENT OF CLAIM

---

1   By a written agreement dated 12 June 1994 made between the plaintiffs and the defendants, the plaintiff agreed to build a loft room and *en suite* bathroom at 74 Mango Walk, Mobay, Sussex, in accordance with planning specifications supplied by the defendant for the total sum of £13,000.

2   The terms of the agreement provided that payments were to be made in stages in that:

(a) £3,000 initial deposit;

(b) £1,000 on the erection of the roof;

(c) £3,000 on completion of the electrical and plumbing works;

(d) £3,000 on erection of the stairs;

(e) £2,000 on completion of the laying of floors;

(f) £1,000 one month after the works are completed.

3   In accordance with the agreement the plaintiff began work on the 5 July 1994 and the £3,000 initial deposit was paid by the defendants to the plaintiff.

4   By an order dated and signed by the Minister of State for Defence, the building was requisitioned by the government for temporary military use until 5 July 1996.

5   As a result of the requisition the performance of the agreement became without any fault on the part of the plaintiffs impossible and the agreement was frustrated and the plaintiffs discharged from further performance of the agreement.

6   For reason of the matters aforesaid the plaintiff has suffered loss, expense and damages.

Particulars

    (a)   Expenses incurred in executing the agreement £

    (b)   Cost of laying the floor as per the agreement £3,000

7 Further the plaintiff claims interest pursuant to s 35a of the Supreme Court Act 1981 on such sums and at such rates as the court sees fit and the plaintiff claims:

    (i)   a declaration that the agreement dated 12 June 1994 was frustrated on the 5 August 1994 by the action of the government in requisitioning the building for defence purposes.

    (ii)   The sum of £   in respect of expenses incurred by the plaintiff to the date of frustration pursuant to s 1(2) of the Law Reform (Frustrated Contracts) Act 1943.

    (iii)   The sum of £3,000 or such sum as the court considers just in respect of valuable benefits obtained by the defendant pursuant to s 1(3) of the Law Reform (Frustrated Contracts) Act 1943.

    (iv)   Damages for breach of contract.

    (v)   Interest pursuant to s 35 of the Supreme Court Act 1981.

B A Barrister
7 Kings Court
Chancery Lane
London W11

8   Remedies: damages

Introduction

The usual common law remedy for breach of a term of a contract is damages (ie monetary compensation). In addition, the breach of contract in a particular instance may be so severe that the injured party is entitled to treat the contract as having reached its end and repudiate it. Alternatively, in less serious cases where it is assessed that only a warranty is breached, damages remain the sole common law remedy.

However, damages are not an entirely satisfactory remedy in all situations and so equity has developed a range of different and alternative remedies to supplement the effectiveness of common law damages. When assessing damages, the normal approach to contractual damages is to put the plaintiff in the position, financially, that he would have been in, had the contract been performed. It is the expectancy relating to this position that the plaintiff be compensated for. It is important to keep in mind the compensatory heart of contractual damages. Assessment of damages should not be driven by punitive desires to make the defendant pay for not keeping his word. Hence in situations where the plaintiff would have made a loss had the contract been performed (because perhaps of a sudden change in the market), they cannot seek compensation from the defendant. And it would not be fair to include in the assessment of compensation a loss which would have been suffered in any event even if the defendant's performance had been proper (*C & P Haulage v Middleton* (1983)). It is clear that no party should make an additional profit from the damages and it should be established that there is loss to the plaintiff in consequence of the breach.

Depending on the circumstances, there are a number of ways in which a party not in breach can be compensated for loss and the plaintiff may usually choose which head of compensation he wishes in a particular case, whether it be: damages for loss of bargain; reliance loss; restitution; or incidental and consequential losses. The plaintiff may combine his claims as he wishes but he may not be compensated twice for the same loss.

Reliance basis

The aim of reliance damages are put the plaintiff in the position he would have been in, if the contract had never been made, by compensating him for his wasted expenditure. In *C & P Haulage v Middleton* (1983), the Court of Appeal held that where the plaintiff had entered what turned out to be a bad bargain, he could receive only nominal reliance damage unless the wasted expenditure was the defendant's fault. However, in such cases the burden is on the defendant to show that the transaction was so unprofitable that the plaintiff's expenses would not be covered. (*CCC Films Ltd v Impact Quadrant Films Ltd* (1984)) Where it is deemed likely that the transaction would have at least covered the plaintiff's expenditure it appears that some pre-contractual expenses may be included. In *Anglia Television v Reed* (1971), a famous film actor failed to play a TV part for which he had been engaged, after repudiating his contract. The Court of Appeal held that Mr Reed was liable to pay the television company's costs in employing a director and a designer to prepare the project.

Restitutionary

Where a bargain is made and the price is paid, and the goods or services contracted for are not forthcoming by reason of the (defendant's) breach, then the plaintiff is entitled to the price paid plus the interest earned in the interim. This applies whenever there is a total failure of consideration.

Consequential/incidental losses

Consequent on any breach of contract may be further losses. The sale of a defective lorry may create many forms of consequent loss, if it means that I am unable to deliver my load or if I injure some one else. Incidental losses are those losses incurred by the plaintiff when he realises the defendant's breach. To use the lorry example again, a prudent haulier may hire a replacement lorry rather than risk not fulfilling his contract or being a danger on the road. Incidental loss would cover that cost plus the costs of sending the lorry back.

Remoteness of damage

There has to be some limit, however, to a defendant's liability in damages after he has breached a contract. The doctrine of remoteness of damage provides that limit. The plaintiff will not be able to recover damages for all the loss suffered if the court adjudges that some of that loss is just too remote a consequence of the breach to be compensated by the defendant. The rule as stated by Baron Alderson in *Hadley v Baxendale* (1854) was that:

> Where two parties have made a contract which one of them has broken, the damages which the other party ought to receive in respect of such breach of contract should be such as may fairly and reasonably be considered as either arising naturally, ie according to the usual course of things, from such breach of contract itself, or such as may reasonably be supposed to have been in the contemplation of the parties at the time they made the contract as the probable result of the breach of it.

This principle has been restated and discussed by the Court of Appeal in *Victoria Laundry (Windsor) Ltd v Newman Industries* (1949) and the House of Lords in *The Heron II* (1967).

The result of this restatement is that it is clear that a plaintiff can recover for such loss that was a 'serious possibility' or a 'real danger' or a 'very substantial probability of loss' as was at the time of contract liable to result from breach (note: the standard is much higher than the tortious level of reasonable foresight in relation to remoteness of damage). While what was foreseeable will depend on the knowledge possessed by the parties at the time, such knowledge may be implied in that every reasonable person is assumed to be aware of certain matters and to be able to forecast the likely consequences of a breach in those circumstances. A person may also have specialist knowledge which is of some special state of affair outside the normal course of things.

In regard to the first limb of Baron Alderson's proposition that a plaintiff may recover for loss arising naturally out of the breach, it is not vital that the parties actually contemplated the natural consequences of the breach but merely that had a reasonable person done so they would have come to the conclusion that the loss in question was a natural consequence of the breach. Further, it need not be proved that the parties must have believe that a breach would inevitably result in a particular form of loss. The test is not whether once a breach occurs the particular loss is inevitable.

In regard to the Baron's second proposition, relating to damages that may be supposed to have been in the contemplation of the parties at the time of contract, actual specialist knowledge as to the risk of the plaintiff suffering abnormal or unusual loss on behalf of a defendant will be enough to deem the loss foreseeable. This does not mean that the defendant is liable for all loss once liability has been found, it must be not only knowledge but acceptance by the defendant of the purpose and intention of the plaintiffs in stressing the importance of the special circumstances. However, once the court has held that a particular type of loss is known about and accepted by the defendant, the loss will not be too remote if its extent was far more serious than could reasonably be foreseen (*H Parsons (Livestock) Ltd* (1978)).

Causation

The fact that the contract is in breach does not prove of itself that the ultimate loss claimed by the plaintiff was caused by the plaintiff was caused by or sustained as a result of the breach. It is clear, however, that where there is a second event actioned by a third party which causes additional loss, or aggravates the existing situation this will not relieve the defendant from his liability. Similarly, the mere fact that there are two alternative causes of loss, one arising from breach of contract an the other not, will not avail the defendant of his responsibility. In *Smith Hogg & Co v Black Sea Insurance Group* (1940) cargo was lost, partly because the ship was unseaworthy. The latter breach could clearly support a claim for damages.

Quantifying damages

In addition to quantifying damages by means of reliance loss, restitution or loss of bargain, it is possible to identify certain heads of loss which although possibly foreseeable are incapable of being recoverable. Such irrecoverable damages are damages for injury to feelings, damages for injury to reputation. Having dealt with those damages that do not qualify for enforcement by the courts, it is time to look at those that do.

Distress and inconvenience

While simple commercial contracts with profit as the sole motive will not attract such awards, cases where the contract itself 'was to provide peace of mind or freedom from distress' (*Bliss v SE Thames RHA* (1987)), a holiday for example, such loss will be recoverable. In *Jarvis v Swan Tours* (1972), a holiday case, the Court of Appeal made it clear that substantial damages may be recovered for disappointment, vexation and mental distress caused by a breach in the holidaymakers' contract. In contrast the House of Lords have refused to allow damages for injury to feelings in a wrongful dismissal case.

Diminution of future prospect

However, where a wrongful breach of contract does not merely cause upset but also may cause the plaintiff to lose his job which in turn may damage his future prospects for employment, then damages for such loss are recoverable. This was the case in *Edward v SOGAT* (1970) where a member of a trade union was wrongfully expelled. Further where such a wrongful breach damages the commercial reputation of an organisation, then such loss can be recovered (*Anglo-Continental Holidays v Typaldos Lines* (1967)).

Speculative damages

In the last resort, where a person cannot put a specific value on his loss, and he has clearly lost the chance of doing something and this contingency was outside the parties' control then if he loses a chance, he should be compensated for the value that chance might have represented.

Mitigation of damages

There is a continuing duty on a plaintiff to act reasonably even when it is the other party who has breached the agreement. If any particular loss suffered by the plaintiff could have been avoided had he taken reasonable steps, then the plaintiff will not be able to claim for such loss. The plaintiff will be compensated by the defendant for taking such steps to try and mitigate his loss even if at the end of the day he is unable to. The general rule remains that the plaintiff should not make a profit on the fact of the breach. Hence if the plaintiff successfully mitigates his loss and obtains any benefits as a result of his efforts, then these must be taken into account when calculating the damages to be paid by the defendant, as the plaintiff cannot recover for any loss that he has avoided. However, it is for the defendant to prove that particular losses resulted from a failure to mitigate.

Liquidated damages

Sometimes the parties to a contract are aware of the potential hazards and breaches they face. They may therefore choose to estimate the damages and likely losses before the breach and incorporate such figures into the contract. Where there is such a 'liquidated damages clause' the courts will not inquire as to the actual losses in a particular case (whether higher or lower) but award the sum stipulated in the contract. Such an agreed damages clause will only be effective in the event of a breach of contract case. However, it is clear that it is a *bona fide* attempt to assess the damages at the formation of contract and not a penalty clause. Penalty clauses are clauses intended as a punishment to frighten a party into completing a contract will not stop the courts looking at the question of unliquidated damages for the actual smaller loss. Whether an individual clause is a penalty clause or not is not a question of its contractual description but of its construction by the courts.

The judgment of Lord Dunedin in *Dunlop v New Garage Co Ltd* (1915) gives guidance as to the construction of such clauses. The tests he suggested to detect penalty clauses were:

> it will be held to be a penalty clause if the sum stipulated for is extravagant and unconscionable in amount in comparison with the greatest loss that could conceivably be proved to have followed from the breach; it will be held to be a penalty if the breach consists only in not paying a sum of money, and the sum stipulated is a sum greater than the sum that ought to have been paid, and there is a presumption (but no more) that it is a penalty clause when a single lump sum is made payable by way of compensation on the occurrence of one or more or all of several events, some of which may occasion serious and others but trifling damage.

On the other had Lord Dunedin felt that:

> as far as identifying liquidated damage clauses that it is an obstacle to the sum stipulated being a genuine pre-estimate of damage, that the consequences of the breach are such as to make precise pre-estimation almost an impossibility. On the contrary, that is just the situation when it is probable that pre-estimated damage was the true bargain between the parties.

In the *Dunlop* case, the plaintiff company had supplied tyres to the defendants subject to an agreement that the defendants would not resell them below their recommended list price. The defendants had to pay £5 'by way of liquidated damages and not as a penalty' for every tyre sold in breach of the agreement. The House of Lords held that this provision was not penal and was in the nature of agreed damages as undercutting would have damaged the plaintiff's business. In such a case precise pre-estimation of the loss was difficult if not impossible and as the sum stipulated in the contract was reasonable in the circumstances the clause would stand. Such a case must be contrasted with the case where a sum of money is to be paid upon the occurrence of an event that is not a breach of contract. In *Alder v Moore* (1961), a professional footballer who had collected insurance money when retiring injured from football and had signed a clause promising to repay the money should he return to the game, was forced to repay the money when he did return to playing football.

Remedies: specific performance

Where there is a breach of contract and it is clear that common law remedies will not suffice, the court may order specific performance if is equitable to do so. Where it is clear that this remedy will create hardship the court will not impose the remedy. In *Patel v Ali* (1984), specific performance was refused of a contract for the sale of a house as the defendant vendor, who spoke little English and had contracted a serious illness, needed to be near friends and relatives. The situations to which specific performance applies are limited.

Adequacy of damages

Specific performance will only be available where damages are a clearly inadequate remedy. It is rare that the courts will exercise the power contained in s 52 of the Sale of Goods Act 1979. It is far more frequently ordered in relation to land as land, is frequently unique and quite irreplaceable by money.

Personal services

Where a contract involves personal services, as for example in the field of employment, it will only be imposed on the employer usually by dint of the Employment Protection Act 1978.

Mutuality

The plaintiff will only be successful if the contract could also be enforced by the defendant. Thus, if there still exists some unperformed obligations which will now never be enforceable, the contract will be lacking in mutuality. The date of the judgment rather than the time of hearing is the relevant time to consider mutuality (*Sutton v Sutton* (1984)).

Constant supervision

The courts will not rule an order where they would be regarded to be in constant supervision of the performance of the contract. In *Ryan v Mutual Tontine Westminster Chambers Assocn* (1893), the Court of Appeal refused to order specific performance where a contract required a resident porter to be in attendance at a block of flats.

Remedies: injunction

There is a general rule that a court in equity will not grant an injunction where its effect would be to compel a party to a contract to do something which could not have been made subject to an order of specific performance. An injunction will usually take one of three forms: an interlocutory, which is granted to regulate the conduct of the parties; prohibitory, orders something not to be done by the defendant; and mandatory, orders not to do something positive, ie to refrain from doing something he had promised not to do. The courts will refrain from imposing personal services contracts unless it is to restrain a breach of a negative stipulation and does not compel performance. A good example of this is *Warner Bros v Nelson* (1937); in this case a well-known film actress had agreed with the plaintiff's film company that she would not act for any other film company for a year. Warner Bros were granted the injunction to prevent her from working for any other film company. The effect of the injunction was to cajole performance rather than to force someone to do a job. The actress was free to earn an income away from the silver screen that year.

Damages in lieu

Section 50 of the Supreme Court Act provides that the court may order payment of damages instead of or in addition to the equitable remedies of specific performance or equity. Since usually where a plaintiff wants damages they will apply under common law, this equitable power has little practical benefit. Where it comes into its own is where the plaintiff has no completed cause of action or needs the assistance of equity to assess damages at the most equitable time in the transaction (and not just at breach as in common law).

Remedies and privity

The general rule of privity is that a person who is not a party to the formation of a contract, can neither sue or be sued on that contract. There are a number of exceptions to the rule.

Common law exceptions

There are a number of statutory exceptions to the privity rule. The best known are: s 11 of the Married Woman's Act 1882, which allows for a spouse to claim the benefit of a life assurance policy taken out by the other spouse; s 136 of the Law of Property Act 1925, which allows the rights under a contract to be assigned; and s 29 of the Bill of Exchange Act 1882, which allows a third party to sue on a cheque or bill of exchange.

In addition, where a principal allows an agent to contract on authority on his behalf, that principal may sue the third parties with which the agent contracts.

Exceptions in equity

There is some authority for the proposition that trusts can be used to evade the privity doctrine. While it is strictly possible to hold the benefit of a contract on trust for a third party, the court will require the trust to be sufficiently certain and not capable of being varied consensually by the trustee and the beneficiaries (*Re Schebsman* (1943)). If a trust is found to exist then the beneficiary can request that the trustee sue the third party and, in the event of refusal, bring proceedings himself (joining the trustee as co-defendant).

CASE SCENARIO

David and Rolin Peemer v Buildwright Construction Ltd

Instructing solicitors act for David and Rolin Peemer. In 1989, both brothers bought a plot of land in Kenley, Surrey, in order to build a go-kart circuit. As David Peemer was a draftsman, he drew up the plans for the circuit himself and obtained the relevant permission from the planning department. The site was made ready for the building works to begin on 17 September 1990. The brothers engaged Buildwright Construction Ltd, a small family-run company, managed and run by Nigel and John Kennedy, a father and son team. The Peemer brothers used this firm because they had done some previous building work for them and they had been very satisfied.

The agreement between the parties was embodied in a written contract dated 30 December 1989. It set out the terms of the agreement and how the work was to be done. It was agreed that the circuit would be complete and handed over on 27 February 1991. The total cost, inclusive of materials and labour was agreed at £140,000.

It would seem that a number of problems arose: the Kennedys had committed themselves to too much work; sub-contractors of unknown repute were used, among other things. The client was five months late in being handed over. This caused great distress and formal loss to the Peemers who were in a chain, ie had to sell their old premises in order to acquire the funds to finance the new scheme. Because of the delay, the purchaser threatened to withdraw, they were then forced to sell at an undervalue and lease premises to retain the goodwill built up, as rival circuits were being opened up in the area. Apparently the Kennedys had no knowledge of these events and nothing was included in the contract to this effect; however, the Kennedys knew about the chain as Messrs Peemer, during the course of various conversations, had mentioned this to the construction firm before the parties signed the contract.

The Peemers accepted handover of the Whizz Co Circuit on 5 August 1992 and immediately realised that much of the work was unsatisfactory. The ground surface was made from a cheaper material than they had contracted for and was not to specification. The windows should have been completely shatterproof with PVC frames. The glass was semi-shatterproof, the walls were not soundproof and needed replacing, the general quality of the work was very poor and the Peemers estimated that it would cost £20,000 to meet the specifications of the contract. They were unable to use the circuit and had to lease, at short notice, a substitute venue, which had to be hastily rebuilt as a make-shift circuit. This place is not as well-located as the new circuit in Kenley and as a result they are losing a lot of goodwill to their rivals. The Peemers owe the Kennedys £20,000 under the contract, and they are claiming this payment in order to finish and remedy defects in the work, as it seems they are in financial difficulties.

Counsel is asked to advise Messrs Peemer on what steps they should take, and if necessary draft any appropriate pleadings to further their claim.

The practical approach

Legal and factual issues

- Whether Buildwright Ltd had knowledge or are deemed to have had knowledge of the issues related to the timely completion of the building works.

- Are any losses suffered by the Peemers recoverable, too remote, reasonable, consequential?

- Breaches: failure to complete on time; infirm nature of work; specifications not as agreed by plan;

- Amount of damages recoverable.

Dramatis personae

- David Peemer and Rolin Peemer – potential joint plaintiffs;

- Buildwright Construction Ltd – potential defendants.

Gaps in instructions: to be requested

- Statements from David and Rolin Peemer;

- Copy of contract between Peemers and Buildwright Construction Ltd;

- Memorandum of times and contents of all conversations;

- Plans drawn up by David Peemer;

- Surveyor's report;

- Estimates;

- Receipts;

- Missing dates from information.

OPINION

David and Rolin Peemer v Buildwright Construction Ltd

1   I am asked to advise David and Rolin Peemer in relation to breaches of contract by Buildwright Construction Ltd who were responsible for building a new go-kart circuit near Kenley in Surrey. It is my opinion that there seems to be a good case against Buildwright for breaches in their failure to complete the work by the agreed date and also the failure to meet the specifications provided by David Peemer's plan. I am told by instructing solicitors that Buildwright Construction Ltd are in financial difficulties; it seems therefore that the success of any proposed action would depend on their ability to pay.

There seems hardly any point in suing a company that may be about to go under. Could those instructing me kindly make a search at Companies House to see whether there is any information that could throw light on the financial position of Buildwright Construction Ltd.

2   The contract

I would be most grateful to those instructing me for a complete copy of the written contract between Buildwright Construction Ltd and the Peemers. It seems that the contract specifically provided that the building works should be completed and handed over on 27 February 1991. The circuit was not completed until 5 August 1992.

Damages may be recovered for the expense and inconvenience resulting from the delay in completion. In order to be successful in their claim, the Peemers will have to establish that Buildwright had knowledge of the Peemers' circumstances of the chain purchase and their need to be installed in their new business premises by the agreed deadline. Could those instructing me kindly send me details of the times, circumstances and contents of any conversations between David and Rolin Peemer and Messrs Kennedy, before the contract was made which would indicate that Buildwright Construction Ltd knew that the circuit must be completed on time. Otherwise the Peemers would be put to trouble, loss of business and goodwill and profit. Based on the evidence provided, it is my view that the Peemers should be able to recover damages for such losses resulting from the delay.

future loss

3   Could instructing solicitors provide me with detailed evidence of the losses which resulted to the Peemers as a result of the delay. This should include the cost of leasing alternative premises, hiring equipment, storage, removal costs, any sums paid to third parties for making the premises suitable for the five-month delay. Invoices and receipts should also be forwarded to me.

4   **Breaches**

Buildwright failed to follow the specification provided in the plan drawn by David Peemer, which was incorporated as a term of the contract, in regard to: laying the ground surface, installing the windows, and the type, sound proofing. I will need to see the specifications provided by David Peemer and also confirmation that at no time were these specifications varied or altered by mutual agreement. I think it would be useful to have an expert inspect the premises and complete a detailed report of what works need to be done to bring the premises up to specification and how long the completion of such work will take.

5   At present, based on the information I have, it is not possible to give a complete and accurate prediction of the amount of damages recoverable. On the figures I have, it is my opinion that a figure somewhere in the region of £60,000 would be awarded; this figure could increase or decrease based on the information and estimates I have requested.

6   I am told that the Peemers owe Buildwright £20,000. They should not pay over this amount or any other sums, as it is likely given the indication I have of Buildwright's financial position, they would not be in a position immediately to pay any damages awarded against them should this matter proceed to litigation. It is my view that Buildwright should be approached to complete and remedy outstanding and defective works, rather than proceed to litigation which could prove costly and time- consuming.

I have attached herewith a draft statement of claim.

                                                                B A Barrister
                                                                7 Kings Court
                                                                Chancery Lane
                                                                London W11

IN THE HIGH COURT OF JUSTICE   199 P No

QUEENS BENCH DIVISION

BETWEEN

David Peemer

Rolin Peemer   *Plaintiffs*

and

Buildwright Construction Ltd   *Defendant*

STATEMENT OF CLAIM

1   By a contract in writing dated 30 December 1989 and made between the
     plaintiffs and the defendant, the defendant agreed to build a go-kart cir-
     cuit at   Kenley, Surrey, in accordance with plans and specifica-
     tions provided by the plaintiffs and to provide all materials for the same
     for the sum of £140,000.

2   By clause   of the said contract, it was expressly provided that the
     said circuit should be constructed in accordance with the plans pro-
     vided by the plaintiffs and using the materials specified therein. By
     clause   of the said contract, the circuit was to be completed and
     handed over to the plaintiffs not later than 27 February 1991.

3   Further, it was an implied term of the contract and/or the defendant
     warranted that it would carry out the said building work with all due
     care, skill and diligence and in a good and workmanlike manner and
     using good and proper materials.

4   Pursuant to the said contract, the defendant began to carry out the said
     work on   .

5   In breach of the said contract, the defendant failed to follow the plans
     and specifications provided therein and/or to execute the said building
     work with all due care, skill and diligence or in a good workmanlike
     manner or with good and proper materials.

Particulars
   (i)   all the windows in the said circuit are semi-shatterproof and not
         completely shatterproof; the said windows are not framed in
         PVC as specified;

   (ii) the floor surface is not laid with the specified material, and is
         unsafe and unsatisfactory;

103

(iii)   the walls are not soundproof as specified;

(iv)   the general quality of the work is poor.

(6)   Further, in breach of the said contract the defendant failed to complete the said circuit until 5 August 1992.

(7)   By reason of the matters aforesaid, the plaintiffs have been put to inconvenience, trouble and expense, have loss of goodwill, profit and have suffered loss and damage.

Particulars of loss

(a)   Cost of replacement windows;

(b)   Cost of removing and replacing floor surface;

(c)   Cost of removing and replacing walls;

(d)   Loss of goodwill;

(e)   Loss of profit;

(f)   Cost of replacement lease;

(g)   Cost of hiring, storing, and removing furniture;

(8)   Further, the plaintiffs claim interest pursuant to s 35A of the Supreme Court Act 1981 on such sums as may be found due to them at such rate and for such period as the court thinks fit.

AND the plaintiffs claim:

(i)   the sum of £   damages;

(ii)   interest as aforesaid pursuant to s 35A of the Supreme Court Act 1981.

B A Barrister
7 Kings Court
Chancery Lane
London W11

9 Illegality, Inequality and Restraint

Illegality and public policy

The courts will not enforce contracts whose purpose is illegal. It is a principle of public policy that no court will lend support to a party who founds his cause of action on an immoral or illegal act (*Holman v Johnson* (1775)). Hence, it should be no surprise that this rule applies not only to agreements that are criminal in intent but also those that are regarded as injurious to society in the wide sense.

The law will not help a person in any way that is a direct or indirect enforcement of rights under contract which is: expressly or by necessary implication forbidden by statute; or if both parties know that although it is *prima facie* legal it can only be performed by illegality; or is intended to be performed illegally. The parties are presumed to know the law and if a contract is *ex facie* legal and yet is performed in an illegal manner, for example the contract may be enforced by a party who had no knowledge of the other's intention to perform diligently. However, in the case of a contract which on the face of it is legal but which is performed in an illegal manner with both parties participating in the illegal performance, neither party can enforce the contract.

Contracts illegal by statute

In some circumstances it is clear that a particular contract is expressly forbidden by a statutory provision. In *Re Mahmoud and Ispahani* (1921), delegated legislation forbade the selling or purchase of linseed without licence. The defendant fraudulently stated that he possessed a licence but was held not liable in an action for non-delivery by the innocent party as the contract was expressly forbidden. In other cases the prohibition may be implied as in *Cope v Rowlands* (1836) where a statute required that a person acting as a stockbroker should obtain a licence or forfeit a fee. The plaintiff did such work without a licence and in the absence of an express provision, the contract was still held to be impliedly illegal since the object of the licence was to protect the public. If, however, the court makes no such implication, it still leaves itself with a general power, based on public policy, to hold those contracts unenforceable which are *ex facie* unlawful, and also to refuse its aid to guilty parties in respect of contracts which to the knowledge of both can only be performed by a contravention of the statute or which though apparently lawful are intended to be performed illegally or for a illegal purpose. A contract will, however, only be declared illegal if the prohibited act is at the centre of performance of it. In *St John Shipping*

Corporation v Joseph Rank (1956) it was decided that a contract for the carriage of goods by sea was not made illegal when the ship's master allowed loading beyond the deadline which was an offence. Similarly, in *Shaw v Groom* (1970), a rent book issued by a landlord failed to provide all the details required by statute this did not prevent the landlord recovering arrears of rent from the tenant. The test would appear to be whether the illegality in the course of performance affects the core of the contract. In *Ashmore, Benson, Pease Co Ltd v AV Dawson Ltd* (1973), the plaintiff contracted with the defendant hauliers to carry a 25 ton load. The defendants used articulated lorries which by law were not permitted to carry more than 20 tons; it was held by the Court of Appeal that even if the contract was unlawful in its inception, it was performed in an unlawful manner, and the plaintiffs (through their transport manager) were aware of the illegality and participated in it. Therefore it was held that the plaintiffs could not succeed in their claim for damages.

Contracts illegal at common law on the grounds of being contrary to public policy

Immoral contracts

In the case of *Pearce v Brooks* (1866) there was a contract between a firm of coach-builders and a prostitute, where the firm hired out a carriage to her. The firm knew that the prostitute intended to use her vehicle as part of her display to attract men. When she fell into arrears with the hire payments, the firm claimed the sum due, as it was held that the contract was unenforceable for illegality.

Contracts prejudicial to administration of justice

As a general rule, a contract which involves a stifling of a prosecution is illegal and becomes a criminal offence when an arrestable offence is concealed (Criminal Law Act s 5(1)).

Contracts tending to promote corruption in public life

In the case of *Parkinson v College of Ambulance Ltd* (1925), the college made false and fraudulent representations to the plaintiff about the possibility of receiving a knighthood after making a donation of £3,000 to the company. It was held that such a contract between the plaintiff and the college was against public policy and therefore illegal; as the parties were *in pari delicto* an action for damages could not be maintained by the plaintiff, nor could he recover money on the grounds that it was had and received by the defendant for his use.

Contracts to defraud, commit tort or crime

Where a claim in tort arose out of a fraudulent contract between the parties, the conduct and relative moral culpability could be relevant in determining whether, as a matter of public policy, the court would take notice of the illegality (*Saunders v Edwards* (1662)). Contracts to commit crime or tort are both void and illegal, for example a contract to rob (*Everet v Williams* (1725)) or a contract to publish a libel (*Apthorp v Neville Co* (1907)). A contract to commit a fraud on a revenue authority is illegal (*Miller v Karlinski* (1945)). As is a contract to commit fraud generally. This was the situation in *Scott v Brown, Doering, McNab Co* (1892), where there was a contract to purchase shares at inflated prices and thereby rig the market.

Effect of illegality

If the contract is illegal as formed, neither party will be able to sue or acquire rights under the contract. Where the contract is illegal as formed the contract is void. Money paid or properly transferred under the contract is not usually recoverable. There are three exceptions to this rule in that: where the parties have participated in the illegal transaction but are not *in pari delicto*, the less guilty party may be allowed to recover; where the plaintiff repents before the illegal purpose has been fully performed, they may be allowed to recover. Collateral contracts to illegal purposes will also be void. In contrast where the contract is lawful as formed but one party intends to exploit the contract to achieve a legal purpose, the innocent party may be allowed to sue on the contract. The guilty party cannot sue on the contract for damages. Money or property transferred by the guilty party cannot be recovered by him unless he can base his action on grounds other than the illegal contract such as a legal collateral contract.

Inequality of bargaining power

Duress

Duress is a common law concept which renders a contract voidable. For duress to be made out, a threat must be perceived which coerces or compels the will. To be capable of giving rise to duress if not the implication of immediate direct physical intimidation, the threat must be illegitimate either by being: a legal wrong; a wrongful threat; or contrary to public policy. In *Pao On v Lau Yiu Long* (1979), Lord Scarman said that in determining whether there was a coercion of the will such that there was no consent, it was material to examine the particular case to see whether the person alleged to have been coerced did or did not protest; whether there was an alternative course open to them at the time; whether they were independently advised and whether, after entering the contract, they took steps to avoid it. There is nothing contrary to principle in recognising economic duress as a factor which may render a contract voidable, provided that the basis of such recognition is that it must always vitiate consent.

However, a party seeking to have a contract set aside for economic duress must be able to show that he repudiated the transaction as soon as the pressure was relaxed. Failure to do so will amount to an affirmation of the contract (*North Ocean Shipping Co v Hyundai Construction Co* (1979)).

Undue influence

The scope of the common law doctrine of duress despite the recent developments in the area of 'economic duress' still remains of comparatively narrow compass. Hence, in equity, the doctrine of undue influence developed allowing contracts or gifts to be set aside whenever improper pressure was brought to bear on a party to carry out such a transaction. The general rule is that the party alleging undue pressure and influence must prove that it was implied. In *Williams v Bayley* (1866), the House of Lords established that a promise to pay money will be set aside if obtained by a threat to prosecute the promisor or his spouse or close relative for a criminal offence. The pressured party must show that they have been disadvantaged (*BCCI v Aboody* (1989)) although once that is done the equitable principle that one should be allowed to retain any benefit arising from his fraud or wrongful act applied (*Allcard v Skinner* (1887)). In certain situations it is clear that a special fiduciary relationship exists between the parties and there is a presumption of undue influence. In such circumstances there is no need to show that there has been undue influence and that it has been exercised. The question as to whether the presumption applies in a given situation is settled by authority. There is authority to show that relationships between parent and child, guardian and ward, religious adviser and disciple, doctor and patient, solicitor and client and trustee and *cestui que trust* are all special fiduciary relationships to which a presumption of undue influence apply. The presumption is not confined to such relationships between the parties that one of them is by reason of the confidence placed in them by the other, which allows him to take unfair advantage of the first. In a case where such a relationship is alleged to exist, the burden of proving that it does exist is on the party seeking to set the contract or gift aside (*Lloyds v Bundy* (1975)). To discharge this burden the influenced party must establish that: there is a fiduciary relationship where one party exercises dominance or there was an abuse of a relationship of confidence (*Goldsworthy v Brickell* (1987)); and that the transaction was disadvantageous to the influenced party (*National Westminster Bank v Morgan* (1983)). Once this burden has been discharged it is up to the party that has benefited from the transaction to rebut the presumption of undue influence.

The presumption of undue influence may be rebutted if the benefiting party can show that the transaction was the result of the 'free exercise of independent will' by the other party. Theirs can be shown if it is established that the other party had independent advice from a competent adviser who has knowledge of the relevant facts.

Restraint of trade clauses and other void contractual terms

Contracts in restraint of trade are ones which contain provision by which one of the parties agrees to suffer a restriction with regard to the carrying on of his trade, or profession or business. All contracts falling with the doctrine are contrary to public policy and therefore *prima facie* are void unless it can be shown that they are reasonable both between the parties and in view of the public interest.

The burden of proving that, as between the parties, the restraint is reasonable, lies on the promise, the burden of showing that as far as the public interest is concerned, the restraint is unreasonable lies on the maker of the contract. The issue of reasonableness refers to what was reasonable at the time of agreement

Contracts of employment

An employer is entitled to the benefit of a restraint clause which prevents the use of confidential information or trade secrets by an employee, apprentice or even a trainee solicitor. In all cases the question that must be asked is:

> What are the interests of the employer that are to be protected, and against whom is he entitled to have them protected. He is undoubtedly entitled to have his interest in his trade secrets protected ... And that protection may be secured by restraining the employee from divulging these secrets or putting them to his own use. He is also entitled not to have his old customers by solicitation or such other means lured away from him. But freedom from all competition *per se* apart from both of these things, he is also not entitled to be protected against. He must be prepared to encounter that even at the hands of a former employee.'

(Lord Atkinson in *Herbert Morris v Saxelby* (1916)).

An employer may protect his business connections if an employee may able subsequently to entice witnesses. In particular, a former employee can be restrained from using a list of customers of his former employer (*Robb v Green* (1895)).

Sale of businesses

When a business is sold, the intangible element of goodwill and trade connections will often be of crucial importance. It is therefore of little surprise that the courts allow more restraints to be lawfully imposed upon the seller of a business to restrict him from future competition than they might in regard of employees. However, there must still be reasonable limits to the clause by which the vendor agrees that he will not set up in competition with the business he has sold to the purchaser. It is clear from *Nordenfelt v Maxim Nordenfelt Guns and Ammunition Co* (1894) that such a clause is only valid in so far as it protects a proprietary interest in regard to the actual business sold.

Exclusive trade agreements

Where there is an arrangement as in *Schroeder Music Publishing Co v Macaulay* (1974), to provide services exclusively for a period of time, such a contract will be void as a restraint of trade if the contract is oppressive and one-sided. Similarly, an agreement where a garage agrees to purchase all its supply of petrol from one company is void as a restraint of trade. However, in such a case all the circumstances must be looked at to determine whether the clause is void or not. In *Esso Petroleum v Harper's Garage (Stourpost)* (1967), a Solus Agreement lasting four and a half years in return for a rebate on the price per gallon was not thought to be a restraint of trade, while a similar agreement relating to a Solus Agreement lasting 21 years was held to be in restraint of trade as it was clearly longer than necessary to protect the oil company's interests and thus unreasonable.

Other void contracts

In addition to contracts which are expressly declared to be void by statute (such as wagering contracts under the 1845 Gaming Act or restrictive trading agreements under the Restrictive Practices Act 1976) and contracts declared to be void on the ground of restraint of trade, there are other contracts that are void at common law on the ground of policy. One such situation is where a contract purports to deprive the courts of the jurisdiction which they would otherwise have, such as the agreement in *Bennett v Bennett* where there was an agreement by a spouse not to apply to the divorce courts for maintenance. Another example is any contract that seeks to diminish the status of marriage such as a one-sided restriction on a person's freedom to marry or the provision of a nuptial agreement to cover for future separation of spouses.

The effect of the contract being void

The effects of the contract or part of it being void are: that it is only void in so far as it contravenes public policy; that the court has the power to excuse the void provisions and enforce the remainder that does not alter the meaning of the contract; and that money paid or property transferred under a void or partially void contract is recoverable if the contract cannot be salvaged.

CASE SCENARIO

Morris Henys v Bradco Ltd

Counsel has herewith a statement from Morris Henys and some correspondence from Bradco Ltd, and is asked to advise generally.

Mr Henys is very distraught after preparing for print, sketches of the Crown jewels for Bradco Ltd, who now inform him that because of a new government regulation, publication and distribution of any impression of the Crown jewels has become illegal.

Counsel will gather the rest of the details from the enclosed bundle.

Statement by Morris Henys

I am a fairly famous artist, specialising in sketching jewellery. In January 1994 I agreed with Bradco Ltd that I would prepare for print for their 1995 calendar a series of sketches of the Crown jewels. Bradco Ltd are a company that specialise in manufacturing calendars with different themes, and as it was the Jubilee Year, they wanted among the other general nature and sport themes, a royalist theme, to be sold to up-market clients. The theme was to be called 'Royal gold'. The fee was agreed at £20,000, £3,000 to be paid in advance. In February, Bradco Ltd sold the printing rights to its subsidiary overseas companies, Ture Carwes Ltd in the Caribbean island of Xamaila for £200,000. When I heard of the gross inflation in price between what I was to be paid and what the copyright would be sold for, I demanded an increase in my fees. Mr Bradshaw of Bradco Ltd refused. Three months later in May, I discovered through a contact in Xamaila that a term of the contract between Bradco Ltd and Ture Carwes was that the first proofs had to be ready for the first run by Summer's Eve, otherwise Ture Carwes would terminate the contract. Summer's Eve was a contract deadline for Bradco Ltd, to be able to compete with the other companies' launch of their first run of royal prints.

When my contact in Xamaila told me this I threatened Bradco that unless my fee and advance were doubled, I would not have the first proofs ready until after the last legal moment prior to Summer's Eve, this would be midnight the night before, which would make publication on Summer's Eve impossible.

Mr Bradshaw agreed to pay the increase I demanded as long as the first proof would be ready as contracted.

In November when I had completed all the work and had the gloss copies ready for delivery to Bradco Ltd, Mr Bradshaw telephoned me to say that his company had just discovered that a government regulation passed late in 1993, meant any distribution to overseas countries had to have the approval of the Home Office or it would be illegal and a criminal offence.

Mr Bradshaw told me that there was no time to obtain consent in order to meet the deadline of Summer's Eve; therefore they could not print the proofs or the calendars in Xamaila. Mr Bradshaw asked me to return the advance of £6,000. I sent in final gloss copies and told Mr Bradshaw that I had kept my side of the contract, and I wanted my outstanding fees of £24,000.

Extract of contract

A contract between Bradco Ltd and Morris Henys:

It is agreed that a sum of £20,000 will be payable, £3,000 to be paid in advance, and the balance of fees on delivery of the final gloss prints of 'Royal Gold' sketches of the Crown Jewels, delivery of which must be made within a reasonable period to enable publication on Summer's Eve.

Cottage Mill
Suffolk
3 March 1994

Dear Mr Henys,

Further to our telephone conversation, I write to confirm that it is agreed that your fees should be increased from £20,000 to £30,000, and your advance from £3,000 to £6,000, the total amount outstanding on final delivery of the prints being £24,000.

Yours sincerely

David Bradshaw

The practical approach

Legal and factual issues

- Is the contract and its inception illegal?

- Can Morris Henys sue Bradco Ltd?

- Does Bradco Ltd have an implied obligation to obtain the relevant government consent prior to the contract?

- Can Bradco Ltd recoup the £6,000 advance paid to Morris Henys?

- The relevance of Henys' threat to Bradco:

  (a) duress; does Morris Henys believe he has reasonable grounds for making the demands to increase his fees?

(b) does he believe that the threats were a proper method of enforcing those demands?

Dramatis personae

- Morris Henys – potential plaintiff in an action against Bradco for the completion of the contract;

- Bradco Ltd – potential defendants;

- Ture Carwes – second plaintiffs in a possible action against Bradco Ltd for breach of contract; however situated overseas; conflict of laws; consideration.

Gaps in instructions: to be requested

- Full copy of contract between Morris Henys and Bradco Ltd;

- Copy of all correspondence between Bradco Co Ltd and Morris Henys;

- Copy of the government regulation 'Prohibitive Export'.

OPINION

Morris Henys v Bradco Ltd

1 I am asked to advise Mr Morris Henys, an artist of some renown as to what course of action he could take against Bradco Ltd, a company manufacturing and publishing calendars. It appears that the printers agreed that Mr Henys should prepare a series of sketches of the Crown jewels for publication in 1995. After the contract was agreed for a fixed sum Mr Henys pressured Bradco Ltd to increase his fees by threatening to make publication to a deadline difficult, though not arguably a breach of contract.

Unfortunately it appears that Bradco Ltd did not know of the existence of a regulation on 'prohibitive export' which prevented them exporting the sketches to Xamaila. They have informed Mr Henys of the position and he is threatening to sue for outstanding fees.

I am asked to consider the various issues in relation to the contract and to advise generally.

2   Illegality

Mr Henys would like to compel Bradco Ltd to perform their part of the contract by accepting the delivered gloss prints and complete payment of outstanding fees. However, as it stands, if Bradco Ltd were to complete the whole chain of the contract, exporting to Xamaila, they would be committing a criminal offence. Any further performance therefore of the contract would be illegal.

The question that now arises is on whose side of the contract does the illegal act fall? Unfortunately instructing solicitors have not sent me a copy of the offending regulation; therefore I am unsure of its exact strictures. It seems clear, however, from the general gist that the illegal act would be the actual exportation of the sketches. However, it is clearly arguable that a contract which prepares to facilitate an illegal act would be treated as illegal. As it stands therefore, it is my view that the contract between Mr Henys and Bradco Ltd could be held to be illegal.

3 Mr Henys' claim under the contract

Mr Henys wants to know whether he is entitled to claim the outstanding fees under the contract. It is my view that he cannot. He may be able to argue that Bradco Ltd implied a term into the contract that any necessary consent would be obtained, in fact that the contract would be legal. It is my opinion that this would not be a successful argument and would not be sustainable.

However, if this matter were to proceed to litigation, one of the questions that will be central to the success of the case is whether the parties acted together in agreeing what was ostensibly an illegal contract, ie acting *in pari delicto*. It is my view that Bradco Ltd as a company engaging in publishing and export should be aware of any legal restrictions on its ability to contract; the onus would be placed squarely on them as being mainly responsible for the illegal contract.

I would be grateful if those instructing me could obtain a further statement from Mr Henys clarifying whether he knew about the government regulation and whether he was in a position to have discovered it.

4   Return of fees paid by Bradco Ltd

There may be a chance that Bradco Ltd could recover the fees paid to Mr Henys in spite of the illegality, if the matter were to proceed to court. The court tends to retain some discretion at arriving at what they see is a just decision in all the circumstances.

It is my opinion that Mr Henys should consider the cost implication of pursuing this matter, and should seriously consider negotiating with Mr Bradshaw, as he could be throwing good money after bad by pursuing an action where the rules are so unpredictable and uncertain.

5   I have not drafted pleadings, but would be happy to do so, if instructed.

B A Barrister
7 Kings Court
Chancery Lane
London W11

10   Case papers and pleadings

This final chapter is comprised of a set of six case papers which illustrate many of the issues that have been discussed in earlier chapters. The aim of this chapter is to allow the students to try their hand at identifying the pertinent issues and writing an opinion. The facts will be gleaned from the relevant papers. The chapter concludes with an assortment of pleadings.

Problem 1

Mary Ross v Harry Aines

Cornish West Press Ltd v Mary Ross

Instructing solicitors act for Mary Ross, an English Literature Professor who had agreed to write a series of short stories for Cornish West Press Ltd. Cornish West Press Ltd discovered Mary Ross after a recommendation by a colleague at the Oxmouth University, Oxbridge, where they both lectured. In September 1990 Cornish West Press approached Mary Ross and the projected stories were discussed. It was envisaged that the project would take one year and comprise two volumes of 250 pages each. Mary Ross and Cornish West Press agreed the terms. Extract of relevant paragraphs are enclosed herewith.

It would appear that Mary Ross was exceptionally busy during late 1990 and 1991 and overlooked the deadline for submission of the draft manuscript. Mary Ross had a brilliant first-class honours student in her class and decided to ask him to ghost-write the volumes. In February 1991 Mary Ross and Harry Aines orally agreed the terms of the contract. Harry Aines was to write the stores and was to be paid 20% of the royalties. Mary Ross stipulated that secrecy about the project was essential. Harry Aines bought a sophisticated computer for £2,500 to work on the project. One month before the deadline for submission Harry Aines rang Mary Ross and told her that he no longer wished to work on the project. A month later two short stories of 250 pages very similar to those agreed by Mary Ross and Harry Aines were launched. Janet Role, the managing editor of Cornish West Press, has written to Mary Ross advising her of pending legal action for misrepresentation and breach of contract. Mary Ross wanted to know what action she could take against Harry Aines and whether Cornish West Press would be successful in any action against her. She has recently discovered that the publishers who published Harry Aines' stories were Cornish West Press Ltd themselves. Counsel is asked to advise generally and draft appropriate pleadings.

Extract of agreement between Mary Rose and Cornish West Press Ltd

The consideration

3 (c)   If the script is delivered after the final date in the script delivery timetable, then the publishers may reject the work and summarily terminate this agreement.

Author's obligations

5 (b)   The author shall submit the work to the publishers within the time stipulated in the first schedule ...

5 (d)   The author shall not without the prior written consent of the publishers, such consent not to be unreasonably withheld, write and or publish in any form any work which might reasonably be considered by the publishers to be likely to affect prejudicially the sales of the work.

Warranties

9 (a)   The author hereby warrants with the publishers and their assignees and their licensees that the author has full power to make this agreement and that the author is or will be the sole author of the work and is or will be the owner of the copyright.

Termination

14   Should the publishers or the author at any time fail to comply with any of the provisions set forth in this agreement within 14 days after written notice from the other party to rectify such failure ... this agreement shall terminate automatically and all rights granted to either party shall thereupon cease without further notice.

Problem 2

Starline Ltd v Evon Ross

Re Mrs Thadine Alexis. Counsel has herewith:
 (i)   Statement of Mrs Thadine Alexis.
 (ii) Copy contract dated 20 June 1991.
 (iii) Copy letter from Evon Ross.

Instructing solicitors act for Mrs Thadine Alexis who is the managing director of a company, Starline Ltd. As counsel will gather from the enclosed documents, Mrs Alexis is in dispute with Evon Ross and wants to compel her to fulfil her obligation to skate in the national ice-skating championship. Counsel is instructed to advise in writing and settle any appropriate pleadings.

Statement by Mrs Thadine Alexis of 21 Royal Farm, Sussex

I met Evon Ross skating at a local ice rink in Sheffield in 1991. She was 16 years old and I realised that she had obvious talent and flair for the sport. It was obvious that she had the potential to become a champion, but she was unemployed and had no drive. She did not know what to do and simply skated to pass the time away. I approached her and discussed the options with her and I persuaded her that she could become professional. I agreed to act as her manager. Within eight months she had become the regional ice skating champion and was definitely on her way to success. One year later she earned £8,000 in prize money.

In 1993 she became third runner up in the UK ice skating championship and won several other tournaments. In the beginning of 1994 she became the UK champion and earned quite a substantial amount through endorsements. In the summer of 1994 Evon told me that she had been approached by another company based in Belgium and was thinking about being managed by someone else. I reminded her that she was under contract to me exclusively for another two years and could not leave without my agreement to discharge the contract. I also reminded her that we had a number of championships coming up later that year. In March of 1994 I received a letter from Evon stating her dissatisfaction with my management and telling me that she had decided to withdraw from our contractual agreement and that she was going to be managed by Alain Defen of the Belgium Warriors.

Management agreement

Made on 20 June 1991 between Starline Ltd, the manager and Evon Ross, the player.

It is hereby agreed as follows:
- (i) that the player will not during the period of this agreement play in any tournament or endorse any product or enter any contract in a professional capacity without the agreement of the manager;
- (ii) that the manager will use her best endeavours to develop the player's career and to obtain sponsorship endorsement and appearance money for the player throughout the period of this agreement;
- (iii) that the player will be managed exclusively and directed in all matters concerned with her career as an ice skater for a period of five years commencing with the date of this agreement;

(iv) the player will pay to the manager or allow the manager to receive or retain 10% of all her gross earnings as an ice skater during the period of this agreement.

Letter from Evon Ross to Thadine Alexis

Dear Thadine

I am so sorry but I have decided not to carry on with our agreement. I have been very dissatisfied with your form of management over the past three years and I have decided that in order for the perfection of my career and the advancement of my career I should in fact go to Europe where my chances are far greater.

Under the circumstances I think it would be better if we parted. I am aware of my contractual obligations, but I am sure that you will agree that it is in our best interest that we both take these steps.

Thank you for all that you have done to enhance my career.

All the best.

Evon

Problem 3

Patsy Rowe v Janus Secuor Ltd

Counsel is instructed on behalf of Patsy Rowe who bought a security system for her home in the quieter parts of Paddock Wood, Wiltshire. Mr Rowe made an agreement with a company, Janus Secuor Ltd, who sold and installed the system. Counsel will gather the facts from the enclosed papers. Counsel is asked to advise Miss Rowe, who is very distressed, and to draft appropriate pleadings.

Statement by Patsy Anne Rowe of Honeycup Cottage, Paddock Wood, Wiltshire

I saw an advertisement in the *Paddock Wood Times* on 10 January 1994 offering security systems for sale at a special price and decided that with the rise of intruders in the area I would buy one. I telephoned Janus Secuor Ltd and spoke to a gentleman who said he would send someone round to explain all the details. On 19 January 1994 Bob Grant arrived and gave me the details of the Wonder Eye Security System. He said it was state-of-the-art. It could sense the presence of an intruder one mile away and would send us a signal to boxes attached around the house. He said it would last for 10 years and did not need servicing because of the high quality of the steel that made up the parts.

He said other things that made the system sound so fantastic and really quite unbelievable. Based on what he told me I decided to buy one. He also seemed to be such a nice young man. He and a partner arrived the next morning, 20 January, to install the Wonder Eye System. They worked quickly and seemed to know exactly what they were doing. They asked me to sign a form. I didn't have my glasses on but they said it was to do with the installation of the system and I paid them £1,500 by cheque. The system worked perfectly for four weeks, then it started to bleep erratically. Last week, five weeks after the installation, I was burgled, and a week later the main switch box of the system caught on fire and burned out the whole of the room where it was installed.

I rang Janus Secuor Ltd but they told me I had signed a contract exempting them from all liability for any malfunction and that if I wanted them to come out I would have to pay a call-out charge and pay for the repairs. I want my money back, because what they told me about the system was simply not true and I need to be compensated for all the damage I have suffered in relation to the burned-out room and the inconvenience I have had. I have also had property stolen when I was burgled and I think the burglary was their fault.

Extract of clause in the contract

The company shall under no circumstances be held responsible for any loss suffered by the customer through burglary, theft or fire. The company exempts all liability on the signing by the customer of this agreement.

Pleadings

Purpose of statement/particulars of claim

Counsel is not always asked to draft pleadings, as it is often the case that the request to write an opinion is a method of exploring to see what the merits of the case are. When counsel is asked to draft, he will have to his aid, books of precedent, to assist him in drafting. This section of the chapter offers some basic suggested precedents in different areas of contract law.

Failure of consideration – recovery of money paid

IN THE MOBAY COUNTY COURT   Case No ....

BETWEEN

Ras Iley   *Plaintiff*

and

Jumbo Records Ltd   *Defendants*

PARTICULARS OF CLAIM

1 By an oral agreement made on or about 20 July 1994 between the plaintiff and the defendants at the defendants' premises in Duke Street, Kingston, and entered in writing by a memorandum dated 20 July 1994, signed by the defendants, the defendants agreed to sell and the plaintiff agreed to buy a 12-stringed electric guitar for the price of £5,000.

2 It was an implied term of the agreement that the defendants were the lawful owners and had legal right to sell the property, at the time the property should pass.

3 On 25 July 1994, the plaintiff paid the agreed purchase price of £5,000.

4 The defendant company was not at any material time or at all the lawful owner of the guitar, and had to right to sell it, and was therefore in breach of the implied terms of the agreement.

5 On 10 August 1994, the plaintiff was obliged to pass to guitar to Ras Marley who were the lawful owners thereof.

6 By reason of the matters aforesaid, the consideration for the payment of the sum of £5,000 has wholly failed. Alternatively, the plaintiff has suffered loss and damage in the amount of the said sum, by the defendants' breach of the implied term.

(7) Further the plaintiff claims interest pursuant to s 69 of the County Courts Act 1984 on the said sum of £5,000 and on the amount found to be due to the plaintiff at such rate and for such period as the court thinks fit.

AND the plaintiff claims:
- (i)   £5,000.
- (ii) Damages.
- (iii) The aforesaid interest pursuant to s 69 of the County Courts Act 1984.

B A Barrister

Dated, etc.

Anticipatory breach – liquidated demand – damages for wasted expenditure

IN THE HIGH COURT OF JUSTICE   1992 B No ....

QUEENS BENCH DIVISION

BETWEEN

Burksans Tyre Limited   *Plaintiffs*

and

Peacocks Frozen Foods Plc   *Defendants*

STATEMENT OF CLAIM

1   The plaintiffs are and were at all material times a company carrying on business as manufacturers of rubber goods.

2   By a written agreement dated 17 December 1989 (the contract) the plaintiffs agreed to manufacture to a design specification and to sell to the defendants and the defendants agreed to buy 20,000 bungy rubbers for plumbing pipes at a price of 35 pence each. The plaintiff will refer to the contract at trial for its full terms and true meaning and effect.

3 It was an express term of the contract:

    (a) that the plaintiffs should make delivery of the prescribed bungy rubbers at the rate of 3,000 per week beginning on or about 10 June 1990;

    (b) that the defendants should make payment in cash within 14 days of delivery of each consignment.

4 Pursuant to the contract the plaintiffs delivered to the defendants three instalments each of 3,000 of the bungy rubbers on 10 June 1990 and on 20 June 1990 respectively.

5 In breach of the contract, the defendants failed to pay the £1,050.00 price of either delivery or any part thereof within 14 days of delivery or at all. In the premises, the defendants are indebted to the plaintiffs in the sum of £2,100.00 being the total price of the said two deliveries.

6 Further or alternatively, in repudiating breach of the contract by letter dated 30 June 1990 sent to the plaintiff, the defendants refused to accept the delivery of further instalments of the bungy rubbers. The plaintiffs accepted this repudiation by letter dated 7 July 1990 sent to the defendants.

7 By reason of the matters aforesaid, the plaintiffs have suffered loss and damage.

Particulars

(a) The cost of specialist machinery installed for the production of bungy rubbers at a cost in excess of £8,000.

(b) The cost of £4,000 unused bungy rubbers, specially designed for the plaintiffs plumbing pipes which are now unsaleable and of no value. £

8 The plaintiffs further claim interest pursuant to s 35A of the Supreme Court Act 1981:

    (i) on the sum of £210,000;

    (ii) on the amount of damages found due the plaintiffs at such rate and for such period as the court thinks fit.

AND the plaintiffs claim

    (i) Under paragraph 5 above £210,000.

    (ii) Under paragraph 7 above, damages.

    (iii) Under paragraph 8 (a) and (b) the aforesaid interest pursuant to s 35A of the Supreme Court Act 1981 to be assessed.

B A Barrister

Served, etc.

Negligent misrepresentation and breach of contract

IN THE MOBAY COUNTY COURT   Case No ....

BETWEEN

Roy Austin	*Plaintiff*
and	
Wonder-plans Limited	*Defendants*

PARTICULARS OF CLAIM

1   The defendants are entertainment and public relations organisers, who published a prospectus outlining their major services, a copy of which was posted to the plaintiff on his request in December 1993, with the intention of inducing the plaintiff to enter into a contract with them for the provision of entertainment services as described in the prospectus.

2   The said prospectus advertised, *inter alia*, services provided and represented that:

  (i)   the company were experts in the planning and marketing of social events;

  (ii)   used only first class hotels;

  (iii)   provided top quality food.

3   In reliance on the said representations and induced thereby, the plaintiff on 3 January 1994, entered into a written contract with the defendants whereby the defendants agreed to provide accommodation and the planning, marketing and presentation of a Regga Festival Annual Ball at the Pegasus Hotel, Kingston, on 17 August 1993, at a price of £3,700.

4   The representations set out in paragraph 2 above were express, alternatively implied terms of the said contract.

5   The plaintiff paid the defendants the said price of £3,700 and requested that the defendants plan, market and present the said social function.

6   In fact the said representations were false and the defendants were in breach of contract in that:

  (i)   the hotel was not of a first class standard;

  (ii)   the planning and marketing were not carried out by the defendants but were sub-contracted out to novices in the field of marketing, and not by experts;

(iii) the food provided was of poor quality and was inadequate to serve the guests.

7 By reason of the matters aforesaid, the plaintiff was sued by a number of the guests for a refund of their entrance fees. In all the circumstances the event was a disaster and as a result the plaintiff has lost his reputation as a first class promoter of social events and has suffered loss and damage.

Particulars of special damage

(a) Refund of entrance fees: £1,180

(b) Legal costs: £950.00

8 Further the plaintiff claims interest pursuant to s 69 of the County Courts Act 1984 on the amount found to be due to the plaintiff at such rate and for such period as the court thinks fit.

AND the plaintiff claims:

(i) Damages.

(ii) The aforesaid interest pursuant to s 69 of the County Courts Act 1984 to be assessed.

B A Barrister

Dated, etc

Exclusion clause

IN THE MOBAY COUNTY COURT   Case No 94/920

BETWEEN

Ruth Williams   *Plaintiff*

and

Robinson Double Glazing Limited   *Defendants*

DEFENCE

---

1 Paragraphs 1 and 2 of the particulars of claim are admitted.

2 It was an express term of the written contract, set out in clause 3, that the defendants should not be liable for any loss or damage arising as a result of works carried out by the defendants, and if any the damage and loss was limited to £250.00.

3 Paragraph 3 of the particulars claim is admitted.

4 Paragraph 4 of the particulars of claim is not admitted.

5 It is denied that the defendants are in breach of the said implied term, or failed to use reasonable care and skill in carrying out the said installation and fitting, as alleged or at all.

6 No admission is made that the plaintiff has suffered the alleged or any loss and damage, or as to the amount thereof.

7 Further or alternatively, the defendants rely on the express term referred to in paragraph 2 hereof.

B A Barrister

Dated, etc

Problem 4

Sarah Brown v Lakehall Council

INSTRUCTIONS TO COUNSEL

Counsel is instructed on behalf of Miss Sarah Brown owner and landlord of premises 248A Haitian Road Lakehall. Miss Brown entered into a three year agreement with Lakehall for the lease of her property.

The term of the lease was fairly successful and no significant problems arose. However it appears that at the end of the lease agreement the Council stopped paying rent, left rubbish in the front and back area of the premises, which caused the Council to issue a notice under the Prevention of Damage By Pets Act 1949. Miss Brown is very angry and wants action to be taken immediately. Counsel is asked to advise Miss Brown on likely success of any action, and what if any remedies are available to her. Counsel will see that I have enclosed copies of correspondence between Miss Brown and the Council.

Counsel is instructed to advise Ms Brown on the merits of the case and to draft appropriate pleadings.

Statement of Sarah Ann Brown,

33 Kempshott Park, Lucea

will say:

In April 1989, I bought a two bedroomed maisonette as an investment, and decided to rent it so it could pay for itself.

A friend told me that she had contacted Lakehall Council and they desperately needed properties to house one parent families on income support. I telephoned and the Council agreed that they would take the property if it suited their needs. They gave me a date for viewing the property.

The Council viewed the property in January 1992 and agreed to take it over in April 1992. They inspected the property and two weeks later they sent me a long lease agreement which I took to my solicitors and signed.

The lease went quite well, they paid the rent into my account directly every quarter, and there were really no problems. They sent me a determination notice, notifying me that the lease would expire and asked me to arrange a date to inspect and accept handback of the property.

I viewed the property on 12 August and was quite appalled at the condition. The beautiful Victorian wallpaper had been replaced with cheap wood chip paper, and the whole place had been painted white.

The bathroom was a mess, tiles were broken, the bathroom mirrors were cracked; and the kitchen was in a devastatingly awful state of disrepair.

I telephoned Faulty Towers, Housing Association who had taken over the lease from Lakehall Council, and told of my dissatisfaction.

They agreed that some of the work needed to be done and arranged a time for me and a housing officer to view the property.

I visited the property again on 11 June with the housing officer and expressed my dissatisfaction. We agreed that Faulty Towers Housing Association would compensate me and I would have the works done.

At that same visit, an estate agent arrived to view the property; he wanted a set of keys for access to show. I asked Mr Cuttington of Faulty Towers whether I could have a set of keys, but made it quite clear that by accepting the keys I was not accepting handback of the property.

He agreed and let me have the keys. A few weeks later I received a letter from Mr Cuttington, referring to handback and the agreed sum in compensation for the works.

Faulty Towers Housing Association withheld rent for a quarter, prior to handback. They eventually paid the rent but in the meantime, I have accrued an enormous overdraft and interest. Furthermore they stopped paying rent from the day Mr Cuttington gave the agent the keys, he said I accepted handback on that day.

I am extremely upset about the whole matter, and would like some action taken straightaway to retrieve my money. I did write to Faulty Towers Housing Association, but they have completely ignored my letters; I also telephoned a number of times, but they never return calls.

Extract of contract

between Sarah Brown of 73 Sheffield Square Westmoreland,and Faulty Towers Housing Association:

Clause 2   THE Landlord lets and the Tenant takes the Premises together with the benefit of any rights and easements reasonably necessary for the proper enjoyment of the Premises together also with the fixtures and fittings listed in the Inventory annexed hereto (if any) for the Term and thenceforth for three months to three months until the tenancy is determined as hereinafter provided at the Rent per annum payable quarterly in advance the first of such payment being made on the date hereof the second payment being an adjustment payment to maintain the quarterly advance and each subsequent payment being made quarterly thereinafter on the usual quarter days being the 25 March June September and December in each year of the Term until the final quarter when payments will be made one month in advance

Clause 3   THE tenant agrees with the Landlord as follows:-

(1)   To pay the rent at the times and in the manner aforesaid

Subsection(3) To keep the interior of the Premises including common parts (if any) and all Landlords fixtures and fittings clean and in good and decorative repair and proper working order consistent with the Schedule of Condition annexed hereto fair wear and tear and damage by accidental fire and other insured risks excepted and at the determination of this Lease shall give back the Premises in a good decorative state equal to that at the commencement of the term consistent with the Tenant's obligation (fair wear and tear expected) hereunder and shall at the Tenant's own expense remove all furniture not belonging to the Landlord and all rubbish save that the Landlord shall be responsible for any outbreak of dry and wet rot, rising or penetrating damp, whether arising from leaks, penetration or failure of the damp-proofing membrane unless such occurrence is the result of the Tenant or occupant's negligence in which case it will be the Tenant's responsibility to put right the defect at its own expense

(5)   To keep the garden at the Premises (if any) in a neat and tidy condition

(7)   To permit the Landlord and his duly authorised agents upon giving reasonable previous notice in writing to the Tenant at all reasonable times to enter upon and to examine the condition of the Premises and to enter with such workmen and appliances as may

be necessary to execute repairs to the Premises or any adjoining premises belonging to the Landlord

(13) To pay the Landlord's surveyor's and solicitor's reasonable costs and charges expenses and fees arising as a result of any default by the tenant of the terms of this lease and any notice under s 146 of the Law of the Property Act 1925 provided that the Landlord has given the Tenant prior written notice of such default which has not been rectified within a reasonable period of time having proper regard to the nature of the default

Clause 5

Subsection (13) At the termination of the lease the property to be returned to the Landlord in the same condition as set out in the initial surveyors report fair wear and tear expected and subject to the clause 5(4) hereof.

(14) It is mutually agreed that at the termination of the lease the Tenant will endeavour to replace excluding floor coverings any damage and or missing ceramic tiles kitchen fittings door furniture or other of the Landlords fixtures and fittings with items or materials identical to those originally provided by the Landlord in the event of identical replacement items or material not being readily available at reasonable modest cost the damaged or missing fixtures and fittings will be renewed or replaced with items of materials of similar quality to the original to the Tenants choice

(15) It is mutually agreed that at the termination of the lease the Tenant will where required redecorate to the standard of the original schedule of condition fair wear and tear expected except where the Landlord has decorative finishes of high quality the Tenant may replace the lesser quality

(16) The Landlord and Tenant agree that any dispute as to the condition state of repair or any other defect is to be resolved by the decision of the independent chartered surveyor who prepared the original schedule of condition or such other chartered surveyor as appointed by the president for the time being of the Royal Institute of Chartered Surveyors acting as a single arbitrator in accordance with the provision of the Arbitration Act 1950 or any statutory modification or re-enactment thereof for the time being in force the costs of the arbitration to be shared equally by the Landlord and Tenant

Dated _____ 198___

-and-

THE LONDON BOROUGH OF LAMBETH

LEASE

relating to

EHS/C/AM

16 February 1994

Miss S Brown
73 Sheffield Square
Westmoreland

Dear Sir/Madam,

Re: NOTICE OF DETERMINATION

Kindly find enclosed a notice of determination of your lease between Lakehall Council and yourselves.

We are legally obliged to inform you that your lease shall expire on 3.5.94. You will be contacted again when the property becomes vacant and subsequently when the property is ready for handback.

I would be grateful if you could return the tear off slip to confirm receipt of this notice.

Yours faithfully,

Jane Austine
Emergency Housing Services

EHS/PSL/LE1

24.2.95

Miss S Brown   Emergency Housing Services
73 Sheffield Square   373-377 Rose Hall
Westmoreland   London 3BT
                                                      Tel: 0171 738 6000
                                                      Fax: 0171 737 1609

Dear Sir/Madam,

Re: NOTICE OF DETERMINATION

Please find enclosed a notice of determination of your lease between Lakehall Council and yourselves.

We are legally obliged to inform you that your lease has expired/shall expire on 7 July 95. You will be contacted again when the property becomes vacant and subsequently when it is ready for handback.

I should be grateful if you would return the tear-off slip to confirm receipt of this notice.

Yours faithfully,

Jane Austine
Emergency Housing Service

Ref: EHS/MT/PSL/APPX1

TO: Miss S Brown

OF: 73 Sheffield Square, Westmoreland, Croydon, Surrey

Lease made the 8th day of July 1992 between

(1) Miss S Brown ('the Landlord') and (2) the London Borough of Lambeth ('the Tenant') relating to 248A Haitian Road, Croydon CR0 2KB.

The Tenant hereby gives notice that it intends to determine the term created by the Lease on or before 7 July 95 and that I will on or before that date deliver up vacant possession of the premises demised by the Lease and requests the Landlord to accept surrender of the Lease.

Signed: ....

For: ....
        (Agent of London Borough of Lakehall under the Lease)

Date: ....

Faulty Towers Housing Association
373 Clapton Road

73 Sheffield Square
Westmoreland

17/3/95

Dear Sir/Madam,

Re: 248A Haitian Road, Croydon

It is my understanding that although you have issued the determination notice, which incidentally has been issued too early and has no provision for being so issued in the terms of the content; you now propose to bring that date forward by months.

I must bring to your attention that at whatever point before the 8th July 1995, you decide to determine the lease you are still liable for full payment up to an including that date. Further, whatever sum is to be paid for dilapidation's must be agreed and paid together with the outstanding rents.

Kindly note that I shall be away until 27th April 95 and will be unable to correspond with you until that date.

I await your response.

Yours sincerely

Sarah B Brown

EHS/ARC

8/6/95

Miss S Brown
73 Sheffield Square
Westmoreland
Croydon,
Surrey

Dear Miss Brown,

Reference: 248A Haitian Road

I write to advise you that the above mentioned property is now ready for handback.

Please would you arrange to meet me outside the property on

<u>Friday, 16 June at 10.30am</u>

It is very important that you keep this appointment, or appoint a representative to attend, as this will be the official handback date of your property. It is also the official date on which the Association will be discharging its duty as Managing Agent for your property and all liabilities will cease to be our responsibility.

Should you fail to attend the keys will be retained in the Association's offices for collection by yourself or an appointed agent.

If you have any queries regarding any of the above matters, please would you contact me on the above number, extension.

Yours sincerely,

Jane Austine
Emergency Housing Services

London Borough of Lakehall

PREVENTION OF DAMAGE BY PESTS ACT, 1949, s 4

NOTICE REQUIRING STEPS TO BE TAKEN TO DESTROY RATS OR MICE OR TO KEEP LAND FREE FROM RATS AND MICE

WHEREAS it appears to the Council of the London Borough of Lakehall (hereinafter referred to as 'the Council') that steps should be taken [for the destruction of rates and/or mice on] [and] [for keeping free from rats and/or mice] the land known as **248A HAITIAN ROAD, CROYDON**.

TAKE NOTICE that the Council do hereby require you within a period of 21 days, ending on the 17th day of July 1995, to take the following steps [for the destruction of rats and/or mice on the said land] [and] [for keeping the said land free from rats and/or mice], that is to say:

SEE SCHEDULE ATTACHED

DATED this 26th day of June 1995

Please reply to:
Environmental Health Department,
Taberner House, Park Lane,
Lakehall, CR9 3BT

SIGNED...
Environmental Health Technician
[SEE NOTES ATTACHED]

London Borough of Lakehall

248A Haitian Road, Lakehall

PREVENTION OF DAMAGE BY PESTS ACT, 1949, s 4

SCHEDULE

1   Remove all materials consisting of household rubbish including card-
     board and incidental materials from the garden which may provide
     attraction to or harbourage, nesting materials and nourishment for rats
     and/or mice.

2   Take all necessary precautions to ensure that the garden is maintained
     in a clean and tidy condition and free from rats and/or mice.

29 June 1995

Mr Cuttington
Faulty Towers Housing Association
373-377 Clapton Road
LONDON
SW9 9BT

Dear Mr Cuttington

RE: 248a Haitian Road, Croydon

Further to our telephone conversation dated 27th June 1995, I write to inform
you of the following outstanding items that need attention before I would be
willing to accept handover:

(i) Broken glass panel on the front double glazed door

(ii) Carpet paint stained

(iii) The wallpaper used to replace the original is considerably cheaper

(iv) The kitchen sink is chipped and very discoloured

(v) The kitchen floor needs replacing

(vi) Tiles in the bathroom at various places are broken

(vii) Various areas of the house remain unpainted and extremely dirty

(viii) Generally I must say that the quality of work is well below the standard and condition handed to you three years ago and I am generally dissatisfied with it.

I am sure you are aware that until handover takes place, the Association is still responsible for the rent as per the terms of the Contract.

I wait to hear from you.

Yours sincerely

Sarah B Brown

EHS/

21 July 1995

Dear Miss Brown,

Re: 248A Haitian Road, Croydon

Following our agreement, I have requested our Finance Section to raise a cheque for £400 in settlement and you should receive this early next week.

Further I have sent a memo to our Rent Section requesting any outstanding rent up to 19 July – the day you accepted the keys – to be paid in the usual way.

From my point of view, this only leaves the front door to be repaired and I hope this will be completed in about one week, when the second set of keys will be sent to you. The rear rubbish is due for clearance on Saturday.

I am pleased it all ended reasonably satisfactorily.

Yours sincerely,

Tony Cuttington
Emergency Housing Service

EHS/TC/AM

4 August 1995

Miss S Brown
73 Sheffield Square
Westmoreland

Faulty Towers Housing Association
373-377 Rose Hall
Clapton Road
SW4

WITHOUT PREJUDICE

Dear Ms Brown

Re: 248A Haitian Rd, Croydon

As you will probably be aware, the front door to the above property was fixed and replaced last Friday, 28 July.

The keys you allowed us to retain were returned to us this week and I have pleasure in sending these by separate cover.

Yours sincerely,

Tony Cuttington
Emergency Housing Service

Faulty Towers Housing Association
373-377 Clapham Rd
London SW9 9BT

Miss S Brown
73 Sheffield Square
Westmoreland

7.8.95

Dear Mr Cuttington,

Re: 248A Haitian Road

Than you for your letter dated 4th August. Further to my conversation with yourself and your manager, Stuart, may I kindly draw your attention to my letters dated 17.3.95 and 29.6.95 and numerous conversations between these dates.

May I further draw your attention to Clause 3 of the tenancy agreement, and ask you to let me have a cheque for rental amounts from the 19.7.95 to 28.7.95

and the sum of £409.35p, as interest and service charges debited to my account, as a result of your breach and default of contract for failure to pay rent.

I will allow you 14 days to take the appropriate action after which I will have no option but to serve the relevant summons in the county court.

Enclosed please find copies of letter, from myself and from my bank.

Yours sincerely

Sarah B Brown

IN THE CROYDON COUNTY COURT   1995 Case No

SARAH BARBARA BROWN   *Plaintiff*

-and-

FAULTY TOWERS HOUSING ASSOCIATION

-and-

ANNE ASHLEY   *Defendants*

PARTICULARS OF CLAIM

---

1   The Plaintiff was at all material times the Landlord of demised premises known as 248a Haitian Road, Croydon CR0 2EB, The Defendants were Tenants under a lease agreement dated April 1992.

2   The terms of the agreement were, *inter alia*, as set out in the lease agreement, by Virtue of Clause 3(1) the Tenants were responsible for paying the rent on the due date.

3   It was an expressed Term of the Agreement that the Defendants should pay the rent at the times and in the manner agreed and that if the plaintiff suffered any detriment as a result of their default, the Defendants should pay the Plaintiff reasonable costs and charges, expenses and fees accruing as a result of any default by the Defendant of the Terms of the Lease.

4   In breach of Clauses 3(1) and 3(15), the Defendants unlawfully withheld rents as a result the Plaintiff suffered loss and damage.

5   By reason of the matters aforesaid the Plaintiff has suffered Loss and damage.

Particulars of loss and damage

(1)   Loss Rent to the value of   150.00

(2)   The Interest incurred on an overdraft penalty
       as a result of non-payment of Rent amount to   <u>409.35</u>
                                                                           <u>559.35</u>

6   Further the Plaintiff claims Interest Pursuant to s 69 of the County Court Act 1984 on the amount of damages found to be done to the Plaintiff at such rate and for such period as the Court thinks fit.

AND the Plaintiff Claims:

(1)   Damages

(2)   Interest

(3)   The aforesaid Interest Pursuant to s 69 the County Court Act 1984 to be assessed.

Dated 20 September 1995   B A Barrister
                                                            7 Kings Walk
                                                                  Temple

Notice of Issue of Default Summons (amount not fixed) **In the CROYDON COUNTY COURT**

Plaintiff
S B BROWN

To the plaintiff's (solicitor)

Sarah Barbara Brown
73 Sheffield Square
Westmoreland

Plaintiff's Ref:

Date: 26 September 1995
The court office is open between 10am and 4pm Monday to Friday

Please bring this notice with you to court

Case Number	Defendant(s)	Issue fee	Date of postal service
CR505510	Faulty Towers Housing Association	70-	5 OCT 95

Notes

• The above case(s) was (were) issued today. The Defendant has 14 days from the date of service to reply to the summons. If the date of postal service is not shown on this form you will be sent a separate notice of service (Form N222).

The defendant may either

• Pay an appropriate amount into court or compensate you. This is called a payment in satisfaction. The court will send you a notice telling you how much has been paid and explaining what you should do next.

• Dispute your claim. The court will send you a copy of the defence and/or counterclaim and will tell you what to do next.

• Admit that he should pay you an appropriate amount in compensation but ask for time to pay. The court will send you a copy of the reply and tell you what to do next.

• Admit liability but make no proposal for payment. The court will send you a copy of the reply and tell you what to do next.

• Not reply at all. You should wait 14 days from the date of service. You can then ask the court to enter judgment by completing Form N234. If you do not ask for judgment within 12 months of the date of service, the case will be struck out. It cannot be reinstated.

• The summons must be served within 4 months of the date of issue or (6 months if leave to serve out of the jurisdiction is granted under Order 8, rule 2). In exceptional circumstances you may apply for this time to be extended provided that you do so before the summons expires.

• **You may be entitled to interest if judgment is entered against the defendant and your claim is for more than £5,000.**

• **Always quote the case number.**

Proceedings after judgment

You must inform the court IMMEDIATELY if you receive any payment while a warrant or other enforcement is current and/or before any hearing date

You should keep a record of any payments you receive from the defendant. If there is a hearing or you wish to take steps to enforce the judgment you will need to satisfy the court about the balance outstanding.

You should keep a record of any payments you receive from the defendant. If there is a hearing or you wish to take steps to enforce the judgment you will need to satisfy the court about the balance outstanding. You should give the defendant a receipt and payment in cash should always be acknowledged.

You should tell the defendant how much he owes if he asks.

N205 Notice of issue default summons (amount not fixed) (Order 3, rule (2)(d)(1))

Noddy Town Bank
Westmoreland
0171 583 6421

Miss S B Brown
73 Sheffield Square
Westmoreland
Croydon Surrey

Your ref:
Our ref: AM/Chafs/4
3 August 1995

Dear Miss Brown,

Account No 0765201

As requested please find listed below interest and charges for period April 1995 to July 1995:

Debit Interest	Service Charges	Credit
£377.35	£32.00	Nil

Please do not hesitate to contact me should you wish to discuss the matter further.

Yours sincerely

B Shenan
Business Banking Manager

EHS/HALS/AM/JB

29/9/94

Miss Brown
73 Sheffield Square
Croydon Surrey

RE: 248a Haitian Road, Croydon

We write with reference to the above named unit which is currently leased by this Association.

Upon visiting the property recently 1994, the following defects were noted:

Further to my colleague's letter 2/2/94:

The water penetration through the bedroom window frames in the upper floor is causing the wood to rot and will cause damage to the plaster.

The fences also require urgent attention.

As a matter of urgency, could you please arrange for a contractor to visit the property to carry out the repairs.

Once an appointment has been arranged with a contractor, please contact me to notify the occupants accordingly.

Jane
Emergency Housing Services

EHS/PSL/LE2

17/5/95

Miss S Brown
73 Sheffield Square
Westmoreland

Dear Miss Brown,

Re: 248A Haitian Road, Croydon:

With reference to the above property, I write to advise you that the premises are now with vacant possession. At present a pre-handback inspection is being carried out by our Maintenance Surveyor and you will shortly be contacted with an appointment for the handover.

I would like to draw your attention to the various clauses in your lease which refer to 'wear and tear' of the decorations, and the writing off of floor coverings over the term of the lease. Please also note that missing or broken fixtures and fittings will be replaced with fittings and fixtures of a similar quality. Your property is being handed back in compliance with the above conditions.

If you have any queries, please contact me at this office on the above number, ext 368.

Yours sincerely,

Jane Austine
Emergency Housing Service

1 September 1995

Ms S Brown   Faulty Towers
73 Sheffield Square   Housing Association
Westmoreland

Dear Ms Brown,

Re: 248A Haitian Road

We are in receipt of your letter dated 7 August 1995.

According to our records, rent payments were authorised on the due dates in accordance with the lease up to 24 May.

Our Finance Section temporarily withheld payment for June as they were aware a handback appointment had been made for 16 June and expected a final payment to be made following that.

As you are aware, you telephoned on 14 June postponing the handback appointment, to which we acceded. Further delays then ensued because you registered dissatisfaction about some of the redecoration, culminating with our meeting on 19 June, when you received the keys. Final payment was then authorised on 28 July for the period 25 May to 19 July.

We consider the delay in the final payment to be reasonable in the circumstances. Should you take a different view, it seems to us that the only possible loss to yourself due to interest charges by your bank would relate to the period of the final payment (ie a maximum of 55 days).

Without prejudice to previous correspondence and discussions, the only costs which we could possibly consider are for interest charges duly calculated by your bank and substantiated by a letter from the manager.

Yours sincerely,

Anne Ashley
Emergency Housing Service

Problem 5

Fay Ann Smith v Wasson Productions

INSTRUCTIONS TO COUNSEL

Instructing solicitors act for Ms Fay Ann Smith. Counsel is instructed on behalf of Ms Fay Ann Smith, promoter and organiser of the world renowned Regga festival; Regga Fun Splash, held in sunny Jamaica. Unfortunately Ms Smith is extremely distressed as the festival had a huge set back this year, because the stage and acoustic equipment which she hired gave her cause for great concern.

Ms Smith had agreed to use a new company Wasso Productions to erect the stage and set up the lighting and provide security guard services for the event.

It seems that this new company failed to arrive on time, erected the stage poorly and in such a way that it collapsed, also provided such poor security service that hundreds of non ticket holders gate crashed.

Ms Smith's business lost thousands of pounds in profit. Ms Smith wants to sue to recover the lost funds. She is also very concerned at what she sees as a loss of reputation.

Counsel will glean the full facts and details of the matter from the enclosed papers.

Statement of Fay Ann Smith

Fay Ann Smith will make statement and say:

I am the promoter and organiser of the annual event Regga Fun Splash. The festival is world renowned and in the past people have come from all over the world to attend, attendance is equally good from the local people. We generally have thousands of people, and the gate takings have been the major source of income for the company netting several thousands pounds.

In the past, I used to use a very old and reputable PR firm, but last year it closed down and moved overseas.

Wasso Productions was a new firm, but it seemed to have been holding its own and had started to build a reputation. I decided to give them a try as it would have been more economically viable to use a local firm rather than contract with an overseas establishment.

I telephoned the office and spoke to a Mr Junior McCall, who identified himself as the manager of Wasso Productions.

We discussed my requirements and exchanged letters.

On 8 August, the day of the festival was due to begin, I telephoned and spoke to Mr McCall again to confirm that everything was ready and that there would be no difficulties.

Mr McCall assured me that everything was ready and that since they were a new firm they had to establish a reputation and this event would give the firm an opportunity to build up that reputation.

It was agreed that Wasso would arrive at about 1pm and have the equipment set up and ready for the 7pm start. We had further agreed how the security guards would be posted around the perimeters of the arena at 5pm to stop any early crashers.

I began to get frantic when at 3pm no one from Wasso Productions arrived and I heard no word. At 6pm a crew of two men arrived. They seemed highly inexperienced and were unsure of what they were to do. They stood about talking for a great deal of time. Eventually they started work, they hurriedly put up the stage, but not before asking if I had any hands that I could lend. I was in such a distressed state it was now thirty five minutes before the gates were to open, and the stage was still in its very preliminary built, there were no security guards to be seen anywhere.

I ended up having to get another firm to come in and help. I paid them what I would have had to pay Wasso Productions, and also had paid a deposit to Wasso Productions.

I have been told that there is a strong probability that I wouldn't be able to promote or organise Regga Fun Splash again; other regular and potential customers have telephoned me to say they are considering whether to allow me to carry on organising and promoting the events.

The night of the 8th of August is a night I shall never forget; with the help of 'Bus It Production Inc' Wasso's two men crew put the stage up. However as they were wiring up the speakers and other equipment, 'Wasso' discovered they were out of electrical leads. It was impossible to get hold of any one from Bus It Productions Inc, they had hired the men, but were closed, so it couldn't hire any other equipment from them. The result was that the wiring was only partially complete, and the sound only distributed to a part of the arena.

Pandemonium broke out in the crowd, there was a stampede to the areas where the sounds were; people were climbing over the walls.

The event was a total disaster.

I want to know what I can do about Wasso Productions and whether I have any rights against them. I still owe Wasso some money and they keep writing to me and telephoning me for the outstanding balance.

IN THE MOBAY COUNTY COURT   Case No

BETWEEN   FAY ANN SMITH   *Plaintiff*

-and-

WASSO PRODUCTIONS   *Defendants*

PARTICULARS OF CLAIM

---

1 The Plaintiff was at all material times the promotions and organising manager of an annual event known as Regga Fun Splash which is held in August
   of each year at Jarrett Park, Montego Bay St James.

2 The Defendants at all material times carry on business, *inter alia*, by hiring
   out acoustics equipment and public speakers providing security service.

3 By an oral agreement made on 16 February 1994 between the Plaintiff and
   Junior McCall on behalf of the Defendants, it was agreed that the Defendants
   would hire to the Plaintiff 50 microphones, 150 speakers, 30 foot cable and
   build a suitable safe wooden platform and deliver the said items on 8
   August 1994, for a total price of £5,000. The said agreement is evidenced in
   part by the Defendant's written Hire Order No 2453.

4 The Defendants were at all material times, aware that the said platform and
   other electrical equipment was required by the Plaintiff for us at the Regga
   Festival and that the festival started on Saturday 8 August 1994 and continued for five days.

5 It was an express term of the contract that the said platform would be suitable, safe and built of sturdy wooden planks.

6 Further, it was a term of the oral contract agreement made on 19 April 1994
   by telephone between the Plaintiff and Junior McCall on behalf of the
   Defendants, and confirmed by the Plaintiff's letter dated 8 June 1994, it was
   agreed that the Defendants would provide a 24 hour security service.

7 It was an implied term of the contract, that the Defendants, their servants or
   agents, would construct the platform with reasonable care and skill, and in a
   safe manner.

8 It was a further implied term of the contract that the security services would
   be carried out with due care and reasonable skill, and in a safe manner.

9 The Plaintiff paid the Defendant's the sum due under the contract on or
   about the 27 June 1994.

10 In breach of the contracts the Defendants their servants or agents

    (1)   failed to deliver or erect the said platform and other equipment on the agreed date but delivered it instead on 8 August 1994 at about 5pm which was approximately two hours before the scheduled commencement of the festival, and finished erecting the platform at about 3am which was about two hours after the festival had started;

    (2)   delivered a stage which was smaller than the one contracted for;

    (3)   delivered only 60 feet of electrical wiring rather than 300 feet contracted for.

11 Further, in breach of the implied term in the contract, the Defendants their servants or agents failed to erect the stage with reasonable care and skill or in a safe manner, in that it collapsed and fell in at about 6am on 8 August whilst being used for the festival.

12 By reason of the said breaches of contract, and each of them the Plaintiff has suffered loss and damage.

Particulars of damage

    (1)   By reason of the late delivery and erection of the stage, the Plaintiff was unable to use the stage for the performing artists between 6am –12 noon and therefore suffered loss of income.

    (2)   By reason of the said failure to provide the requisite length of electrical wiring the acoustics was very poor and the Plaintiff suffered loss of income by having to return 70% gate takings from dissatisfied ticket holders.

    (3)   By reason of the said failure properly and/or safely to erect the said stage, and its subsequent collapse, the number of performances were thereby reduced as a result of which the Plaintiff lost income.

    (4)   The Plaintiff claims lost income from the festival of £25,000.

13 Further, by reason of the matters aforesaid, the reputation of the festival has been damaged and its liability to raise funds in future years has been diminished.

14 The Plaintiff further claims interest pursuant to s 69 of the County Courts Act 1984 on the amounts found to be due to the Plaintiff, at such rate, and for such period as the Court shall deem fit.

AND the Plaintiff claims:

1 Damages.

2 The aforesaid interest pursuant to s 69 of the County Courts Act 1984 to be assessed.

B A Barrister
7 Kings Walk
Chancery Lane
London WCR

Dated etc.

Fay Ann Smith   *Plaintiff*

-and-

Wasso Productions   *Defendants*

DEFENCE

---

1 By an oral agreement made on the   day of 1994 between the Plaintiff and the Defendant, it was agreed that the agreement referred to in the Particulars of Claim should be varied in the following respects: namely

(a) that the time for the delivery of the electrical equipment should be extended until   day of 1994;

(b) that the price of the said contract was to be varied to take account of the agreed extended arrival of the Defendants.

2 Paragraphs 1 and 2 of the Particulars of Claim are admitted.

3 No admissions are made as to paragraphs 3 and 4 of the Particulars of Claim.

4 Paragraph 5 of the Particulars of Claim is denied.

5 No admissions are made as to paragraph 6 of the Particulars of Claim.

6 No admissions are made as to paragraph 7 and 8 of the Particulars of Claim.

7 Paragraphs 9 and 10 of the Particulars of Claim are denied.

8 No admissions are made as to paragraph 11 of the Statement of Claim.

9 No admissions are made as to loss or damage.

Dated   Ian Counsel

Problem 6

INSTRUCTIONS TO COUNSEL

Maria Channer v Lucy Monroe

Instructing Solicitors act for Ms Channer a dually qualified Barrister, and Attorney-at-Law. Counsel may well be able to empathise with Ms Channer. It seem that Ms Channer acted for a client in Jamaica and agreed by way of a promissory note to recover her fees and money put up to complete a sales agreement, in England when the parties returned to the UK. Mrs Monroe has reneged on her agreement and Ms Channer started proceedings herself, but has now become too busy and has passed matters on to Instructing Solicitors. Counsel will gather the facts from the papers.

Counsel has herewith:

1   Statement of Lucy Monroe

2   Various correspondence

3   Various documents.

Counsel is asked to advise generally, and on the strength of the case.

IN THE BRIXHAM COUNTY COURT   Case No

BETWEEN

<table>
<tr><td style="text-align:center">Maria Mia Channer</td><td style="text-align:right">Plaintiff</td></tr>
<tr><td style="text-align:center">-and-</td><td></td></tr>
<tr><td style="text-align:center">Lucy Monroe</td><td style="text-align:right">Defendant</td></tr>
</table>

PARTICULARS OF CLAIM

1   The Plaintiff is and was at all material times a registered and practising Attorney at Law, in St. James, Montego Bay, Jamaica. The Defendant was a client attending the offices of the Plaintiff.

2   By a written agreement in the form of a promissory note the Defendant agreed to pay the Plaintiff the sum of £5,039 for legal services rendered, and repay sums paid to various parties on her behalf.

3   It was a term of the agreement that the Defendant would pay the Plaintiff the sum agreed on return to the United Kingdom.

4   In breach of the terms of the contract the Defendant refused to honour the agreement.

5   By reason of the said breach of contract the Plaintiff has suffered loss and damage.

6   **Particulars of damage**

    (i)   Loss of professional fees.

   (ii)   Interest payable thereon.

7   Further the Plaintiff claims interest pursuant to s 69 of the County Court Act 1984 on the amount found due to the Plaintiff at such rate and for such period as the court thinks fit.

AND the Plaintiff Claims:

   (1)   Damages for breach of contract.

   (2)   Repayment of the outstanding professional fees under the agreement.

   (3)   The aforesaid interest pursuant to s 69 of the County Court Act 1984 to be assessed.

Served etc

B A Barrister
9 Kings Walk
Chancery Lane

Maria Channer will make statement and say:

On 27 August 1992 Mrs Monroe, her daughter and son-in-law visited my Brixham Street office, having been send by New World Realters, to enquire about the speed and procedure of a potential transaction, ie, the purchase of a property Lot 19 Paradise Crescent St James. This was explained, together with the circumstances of my practice, ie, that I was a part-time practitioner linked to F Tichbourne & C.'s firm, and that I was due to leave on 20 September.

On 3 September Mrs Monroe attended at the Gloucester Avenue offices again in the same company of her daughter and son-in-law to give instructions regarding the conveyance of the above property. Mrs Monroe was seen by myself and a colleague Miss Marion Rose-Green – we both took instruction. Miss Rose-Green was to follow up any outstanding matter on my departure.

Mrs Monroe's instructions were:

(i)   to deal with the conveyance of 19 Paradise Crescent, St James

(ii) to draft a lease for the vendors to remain in the property for 3-6 months after the sale as tenants

(iii) to find new tenants on expiry of the lease, manage, supervise and maintain the property and collect rents.

It was explained to Mrs Monroe that it was the firm's policy that for such instructions of overseas clients a retainer was to be left in a client account to carry out said instructions; such amount being £2,500. On the 3 September Mrs Monroe left a deposit of £15,000, being a portion of the deposit on the property.

On 9th September Mrs Monroe visited the Street office and asked whether it would be possible to return her deposit as she had other transactions which needed urgent attention – she further asked whether I would give an undertaking on her behalf to the vendor's attorney – until the arrival of further funds from the UK.

I agreed to this – receipt of amount refunded enclosed.

I indicated to Mrs Monroe that if there was a delay in the arrival of further funds, her completion would be dealt with by Miss Rose-Green – she indicated that she preferred if I completed and she would be willing to stand the cost of any cancellation and rebooking fees for my flight back to the UK.

On 23 September Mrs Monroe attended the Brixham Street office with a sterling draft of £35,000 to completion. The Jamaican dollar which was rated around J$40-42 against the pound, during Mrs Monroe's negotiations with the vendors, fell sharply from $40-42 as a result of the devaluation of the pound in the UK on black Wednesday; Mrs Monroe therefore found herself short of £5,000. I must point out that Mrs Monroe had in fact an additional £16,000 in the form of a sterling bank draft in her possession on that date which she said was committed and she could not use. She then asked whether I could make up the difference of £5,000 and pay her insurance of £200.00 until her return to the UK.

I agreed to this on the condition that she sign an IOU, witnessed by my receptionist Miss Fay Smith.

On the 23rd I transferred the equivalent of £4,600 in Jamaican dollars from a personal account into a client account for Mrs Monroe, in anticipation of being refunded – and made up the difference with a sterling cheque to Bank of Nova Scotia. Since no refund has been forthcoming, I have had to send £4,600 to the Bank of Nova Scotia to cover my overdrawn personal account; transfer receipts enclosed.

The conveyance was duly carried out – copy letters enclosed as to the course of the transactions, also indicating the speed of same. Missing from the bundle are copies of the sales agreement, and transfer, and all documents relating to the closure of the transaction. These documents were given to Mrs Monroe for delivery to me on her arrival in the UK, by the vendor's Attorney; she has refused to deliver them up.

Mrs Monroe has now reneged on her agreement and refuses to pay – to date instruction in relation to the rental (rent is being collected) is still being carried out by Miss Rose-Green of the Firm: to date Mrs Monroe has not formally withdrawn instructions.

The statement of account enclosed is complete in relation to the transaction of the completion of the conveyance of Lot 19, Paradise Crescent, St James but does not deal with the costs in relation to instructions (iii), ie, to find new tenants on expiry of the lease, manage, supervise and maintain the property and collect rents.

12 October 1992

Your Ref: SJ/KP/MONROE

Dear Madam,

RE: MRS MONROE

Thank you for your letter dated 7 October 1992. I am in receipt of your letter and your cheque for £1,300.00, leaving a balance of £4,539.00.

Mrs Monroe instructed this firm on 3 September 1992, in the matter of the purchase and conveyance of Lot 19 Paradise Crescent and further on 14 September in the matter of preparing and drafting a lease indicating that the vendors would become tenants on the sale of the property, further that the firm should manage, maintain oversee the property, collecting rent, finding new tenants and drafting appropriate documents etc.

At the outset it was made quite clear to Mrs Monroe that a retainer which was a percentage of the purchase price of the property was required and would be placed into an escrow account out of which costs as they arose would be deducted; as both sets of instructions were linked, then the retainer would have to be a sum to reflect those instructions. It is a policy that overseas clients leave enough funds to service instructions – and no instructions would be followed until such funds were paid.

The devaluation of the pound against the Jamaican dollar, put Mrs Monroe in difficulty and she had a shortfall of £4,700.00 to make up re her escrow account and £1,139.00, re her costs for the purchase; and £212.00 for insurance.

In an unprecedented act on my part £35,000 to transact other amounts, of £5,839.00 on Mrs Monroe's reliance of a signed promissory note (attached) refund such sums on 2nd October.

You are free to seek legal advice here to satisfy yourself.

My services are herewith withdrawn since you have decided to behave in this dishonest way.

On my return to Jamaica later next month I will draw up your statement of account and this together with the 'I owe you' that you signed will be evidence for the court.

Yours sincerely

Maria Channer

Williams & Co
Solicitors

Maria Channer
94 North Anston
Woodbridge
Surrey CR7 8QJ

Dear Ms Channer,

Lucy Monroe

Thank you for your letter of 9th November.

I am conducting my own investigations into the jurisdiction point and will revert to you. However, I know that you have views on it already: if you would like to let me have the benefit of your existing, considered, opinion it would certainly be welcome!

Assuming that there is no difficulty on the jurisdiction point then it is my belief that you should apply for summary judgment under Order 9 r 14 of the County Court Rules. That needs an Affidavit in support which I will be drafting in due course. Like any Affidavit, it needs to tell a story: it would have to relate to the history of the conveyancing transaction out in Jamaica, the circumstances leading up to the signing of the IOU and in this particular instance also deal with the statement of account.

Are you able to produce a statement of account showing the money received, money spent and the money still due to you?

Secondly, I note that there is no copy of the Summons in my papers. Have you got a copy of the Summons and Particulars of Claim you could let me have?

Thirdly, I would much appreciate a statement from you. I realise that a considerable part of the history can be judged from documents but I need a statement accurately to be able to prepare you Affidavit.

I am letting Messrs. Hampter & Co. Know that you have instructed me. Once I have the Brixham County Court number I will put myself on the record.

So far as the venue is concerned the case will have been transferred to Barnet under the Automatic Transfer Regulations. These allow for a case to be transferred to the Defendant's home County Court automatically on the filing of any Defence. Of course it is possible to argue in certain instances for a case to be transferred back to the issuing County Court, but that would have to be if there was a merit in the argument. Apart from convenience to you and I there is no real argument for saying the case should be at Croydon County Court. I am asking Messrs. Hampter & Company whether they would agree voluntarily to the matter being transferred back to Croydon: after all, Barnet is hardly convenient for them either. If they disagree, however, the case will have to remain at Barnet.

Finally, I note from one of the letters I read you mentioned that you are returning to Jamaica soon. I would obviously like to know what your movements are to be.

Yours sincerely,

M J Wells

Hampter & Co
Solicitors

Maria Channer
94 North Anston
Woodbridge
Surrey CR7 8QJ

Dear Madam,

RE: MRS L MONROE

Thank you for your letter of 3 September. We do not consider that you are entitled to Judgement by Default as we have served you with the Defence. The allegations made in the Defence established quite clearly triable issues. In the circumstances no useful purpose would be served by making an application for Summary Judgement as the same would be resisted.

As we have not heard from you we have today made an application to the Court to consider the question of Jurisdiction and a Statement of Account with supporting vouchers.

Yours faithfully

Hampter & Co

24 November 1992

Mr M J Wells
Williams & Co Solicitors
44 Woodcote Road
Surbiton
Surrey
SM6 0NW

Dear Mr Wells,

Lucy Monroe

Thank you for your letter dated 20 November.

1   Unfortunately I did not keep a copy of the summons. It was a standard one filled in at the Croydon County Court. The particulars said that the money was lent to the Defendant with the express agreement that the amount would be repaid on the date shown in the IOU, in sterling, in the UK: Monies were for fees and a loan.

It is my opinion that there is no issue on jurisdiction; the law is quite clear as to when the English courts have jurisdiction on cases with a foreign element:

(a)   presence of the Defendant within the jurisdiction

(b)   Submission of the Defendant to the jurisdiction.

In my view both of the above are satisfied. Mrs Monroe is present within the jurisdiction, and has indeed submitted to it by accepting through her solicitors a properly served writ.

In Baroda of Wilderstein **(1972)**

The Defendant who was American, made a contact with an American Plaintiff in France to be governed by French law. The Defendant came to England for the day to go to the races at Ascot and was served with a writ. It was held that the Defendant's presence here however temporary was a sufficient basis for the legal serving of a writ.

In relation to the contract between Mrs Monroe and myself, the subject of the contract was a loan/fees repayment of which was to be performed in England in sterling, and not the conveyance and any instruction relating thereto.

3 Copy statement is produced showing balance owed regarding conveyance, etc., is £2,039. Balance owing is £2,500, on account out of which fees are owing relating to instructions carried out regarding the lease and management of Lot 19, Paradise Crescent, St James; the amount of which I cannot ascertain until my return in December.

4 I enclose vouchers for monies sent to Bank of Nova Scotia and other documents dealing with the transactions. Should you need any further details I will be happy to clarify.

I enclose a copy of the relevant section of the Jamaican Conveyance Law; I also enclose letter received from Hampter & Company.

I leave for Jamaica on 12 December, and return on 16 January.

Yours sincerely

Maria Channer

Williams & Co
Solicitors

Miss Maria Channer
94 North Anston
Woodbridge
Surrey
CR7 8QJ

29th April 1993

Dear Miss Channer,

Lily Monroe

I am sorry we were not able to meet on 27 April: if it is any consolation to you, you were not the only client who had to telephone apologising that day in identical circumstances!

I enclose a copy of the affidavit which I have prepared in draft although I do very much hasten to underline and emphasise the word 'draft'. You may well have additional information/comments/amendments you would wish to make. Perhaps if might help if I set out some of my own concerns, namely:-

i)   I am not entirely sure whether you accepted the £1,300 payment on account of the £5,839 and therefore whether the balance of the claim has been reduced to £4,539;

ii)   I have exhibited Miss Smith's affidavit rather than proposing to file the affidavit as a separate document in view of the fact that presumably there is no possibility of her coming to this jurisdiction to be cross-examined on the affidavit. I would at least like to see the affidavit exhibited to your affidavit than not before the court at all;

iii)   unless you have any strong views, I would not propose putting in Dennis Hamilton's affidavit at all for it really speaks of your bona-fides without actually going into the issues involved in the case;

iv)   my main concern is on the statement of account.

Reflecting on my draft I think it would help if I showed that the £5,839 comprised the £4,700 shortfall on the escrow account and £1,139 in respect of Mrs Monroe's costs of the purchase. Your letter to Messrs Hampter & Co, then went on, on 12 October, to mention £212 for insurance. To be frank, even I would say the figure work becomes a little confusing. As you know, I can speak wearing both hats: if you affidavit is to work and is to show that the defence is a sham absolutely then I think it needs to be a wholly intelligible document. When I initially drafted the affidavit I was proposing exhibiting your statement of account as exhibit 'MMC3' but I wonder whether we actually ought to go one stage further. Is it possible to produce a statement of account that shows precisely what money was received from Mrs Monroe, what money, therefore, you had to lend her, what fees have been incurred etc., so that it is plainly obvious to anyone reading the statement of account that you are still owed £4,539 and that other costs are also due? The problem with your statement of account is that it shows £2,039 as due. It is not entirely clear whether that is in addition to what is due to you; a District Judge with a heavy list might think that it means that instead of owing £4,539 Mrs Monroe only owes £2,039. Alternatively it might encourage him to think that she is at least due a better set of account than those which she has had to date. A problem, for instance, with your present account is that, in arriving at the balance due in respect of the purchase price – a balance of £135-14 – it actually fails to show what money was actually provided by Mrs Monroe and what monies you therefore lent to top up what was required. There are also other minor points of criticism on the statement of account: for instance, was the purchase price J$,300,000 rather than J$1,300? I also find it difficult to understand how the balance due on the sale price of £135-14 actually arises.

I am sorry to criticise the statement of account but that clearly is the weakness in your case. There is no difficulty in proving that the promissory notes was executed; equally there is no difficulty in meeting the jurisdiction point. The are of dispute is the statement of account. Under Order 9 r 14 in the County Court Rules one has effectively the same situation as in the High Court, namely the need to prove no triable issue. County court district judges are I think more lenient to defendants than High Court Masters; if a district judge cannot himself see that the money is still due and owing and does not have before him a comprehensive and comprehensible account Mrs Monroe might just defeat the applications for summary judgment.

In case you do not have it to hand I am enclosing a copy of your statement of account as well as my initial draft of your affidavit.

Yours sincerely,

M J Wells

94 North Anston
Woodbridge
Surrey
CR7 8QJ

Mr M J Wells
Williams & Co Solicitors
44 Woodcote Road
Surbiton
Surrey
SM6 0NW

7 May 1993

Dear Mr Wells,

Lily Monroe

Thank you for your letter of 29 April 1993.

I will answer your concerns seriatim.

(i) The sum of £1,300 was paid on account on 7 October 1992. The outstanding balance is therefore £2,539.00.

(ii) I have no objection to which affidavit you use, and bow to your experience in these matters.

(iii)   As above.

(iv)   Please find enclosed amended statement of account.

Also enclosed is a letter from Lily Monroe which bears her signature which evidences her instructions to Miss Rose Green regarding the lease and collection of rents. This may be relevant information to include in my affidavit.

I also attach to this letter amendments to my draft affidavit where the sums of money are referred to.

I look forward to hearing from you soon.

Yours sincerely,

Maria Channer

Enc (2)

14C Melrose Street

To: Maria Mia Channer

Account No_____

Mrs M Monroe

Re: Purchase of Lot 26 Rose, Walk Crescent, St James

Fees incurred

	J$		£	
Purchase price freehold	1,300,000	00	35,135	14
One half stamp duty	35,745	00	966	08
One half registration fee	1,300	50	35	15
One half contract costs	1,000	00	27	03
Tri forms, letter of possession, letter to Natural Water Commission, courier service etc.	1,500	00	40	54
General Consumption Tax 10%	912	00	24	65
Insurance and stamp duty	7,825	00	211	49
Attorney's costs re conveyancing	17,441	43	471	39
Attorney's costs re drafting and executing of lease	17,441	43	471	39
Cancellation fee for flight Virgin Atlantic 20 Sept 1992	2,775	00	75	00
Telephone calls	1,665	00	45	00
Letters @ £9/Faxes	1,332	00	36	00
Conferences x 10 @ £28.50				
Taking instructions re lease, negotiations with other side re rental; re reduction of other side's Attorney's costs, conferences to telephone UK; time spent at Nova Scotia Bank re financial transactions	10,545	00	285	00
Federal Express and courier	2,405	00	65	00
Search on Land Registry/Air courier and Kingston agent	6,600	00	180	00
Engrossment fee for lease	2,200	00	60	00
Financial Services Bank of Nova Scotia Expediting clearance of funds: cheque numbers Halifax Building Society Sort Code 11-97-00 # 008740 £10,360				
# 008741 £4,640	2,775	00	75	00
TOTAL	1,413,462	30	38,203	86

14C Melrose Street

To: Maria Mia Channer

Account No_____

Mrs M Monroe Page 2	J$		£	
Monies lent				
on 25/9/92	5,000	00	135	14
In Escrow Account				
As per instructions to Miss Rose Green			500	00
Balance			38,839	00
Monies received				
Towards purchase price of freehold on 7/10/92			35,000	00
			1,300	00
TOTAL			36,300	00
Remaining balance outstanding			2,539	00

Amendments to Affidavit

7 The actual promissory note itself is now produced and shown to me marked 'MMC 2'. That promissory note was for a total of £5,839 which it was agreed the Defendant would pay me by 2 October, 1992. That she has failed to do in the sum due. The sum of £1,300 was paid on 7 October 1992.

9 Paragraph 3 of the defence says that despite repeated requests I have allegedly failed to produce a properly authenticated statement of account. Such a statement is now produced and shown to me marked 'MMC 3' and shows a balance owing of £2,539 broken down as follows:

Monies lent towards purchase price	£ 135.14
Monies in Escrow Account	£ 500.00
Outstanding legal costs, disbursements etc.	£1,903.86

10 Delete.

1st Affidavit/Plaintiff

Maria Channer

Sworn: 1993

Filed: 1993

Case No

IN THE BRIXHAM COUNTY COURT

B E T W E E N

MARIA MIA CHANNER   *Plaintiff*

-and-

LUCY MONROE   *Defendant*

I, MARIA MIA CHANNER of 94 North Anston, Woodbridge, Surrey, CR7 8QJ Barrister at Law **MAKE OATH** and say as follows:

1   I am the above-named Plaintiff. I depose to this affidavit in support of my application for summary judgment against the Defendant pursuant to Order 9 r 14 of the County Court Rules. The defence filed in this action is a sham.

2   As well as being a Barrister at Law and Lecturer I am also an attorney at law with a part-time conveyancing practice at two offices in Jamaica.

3   On 27 August 1992 the Defendant, her daughter and son-in-law visited my Melrose Street, Montego Bay, Jamaica office to enquire about the speed and procedure for a potential transaction, ie the purchase of Lot 19 Paradise Crescent, St James, Jamaica.

4   On 3 September, 1992 Mrs Monroe attended at my practice's Gloucester Avenue, Jamaica office, again accompanied by her daughter and son-in-law. She gave me instructions to represent her in the property acquisition. Those instructions were in essence to deal with the conveyancing of 19 Paradise Crescent, to draft a lease for the vendors to remain in occupation for some three to six months after their sale of the property to the Defendant and thirdly to find new tenants once vacant possession had been obtained as well as to maintain the property and collect in the rents.

5   On 23 September, 1992 the Defendant attended the Melrose Street office with a sterling draft of £35,000 to complete the transaction. The Jamaican dollar had fallen sharply as a result of the sterling devaluation in September 1992: as a result the Defendant found herself with a shortfall of about £5,000. The

Defendant, on 23 September, had an additional £16,000 on her person in the form of a sterling bank draft but she said that that was committed for other expenditure and could not be made available. She asked me whether I could make up the difference of £5,000 and pay her insurance of £200 until her return to the United Kingdom.

6. I agreed to advance the necessary monies to her provided the Defendant signed a promissory note witnessed by my receptionist, Miss Fay Smith. Miss Smith has deposed to an affidavit confirming that she witnessed the Defendant sign the IOU on 25 September, 1992: the affidavit is produced and shown to me marked 'MMC 1'.

7. The actual promissory note itself is now produced and shown to me marked 'MMC 2'. That promissory note was for a total of £5,839 which it was agreed the Defendant would pay me by 2 October 1992. That she has failed to do in the sum due. On 7 October 1992 I was paid instead the part sum of £1,500.

8. Paragraph 1 of the defence denies any indebtedness and paragraph 2 denies that the Defendant gave me a promissory note. I believe the above shows clearly that those paragraphs are of no substance and are a sham.

9. Paragraph 3 of the defence says that despite repeated requests I have allegedly failed to produce a properly authenticated statement of account. Such a statement is now produced and shown to me marked 'CAR 3' and shows a balance owing of £2,539 broken down as follows:

Monies lent towards purchase price	£ 135.14
Monies in Escrow Account	£ 500.00
Outstanding legal costs, disbursements etc.	£1,903.86
Disbursements etc.	£2,539.00

10 That balance due of £2,539 is still due and unpaid on the promissory note. Has £1,300 been paid? – see letter 7 October 1992.

11 Paragraph 4 of the defence avers that the Court has now jurisdiction in this matter as the conveyancing transaction was carried out under the laws of Jamaica. That is so but the English courts do have jurisdiction for two reasons, namely:

    (i)   both the Defendant and I are resident within the jurisdiction of the English courts, and;

(ii)   in filing a defence the Defendant has herself admitted to the jurisdiction of the English courts.

11 The latter point is not something to be found in the County Court Rules but
assistance is to be found in the Rules of the Supreme Court accordingly
imported into the County Court Rules by virtue of s 76 of the County Courts
Act 1984.

12 RSC Order 12 r 8(7) makes it quite clear that by having filed a defence there
has been a submission to the jurisdiction, if indeed it were necessary for the
Defendant who is within the jurisdiction to submit to the jurisdiction of the
English courts.

13 I accordingly apply for summary judgment as against the Defendant.

SWORN at   )

in the County of   )

this   day of   1993   )

                             Before me,

                    A Solicitor/Commissioner for Oaths

IN THE BRIXHAM COUNTY COURT   Case No 92 12657

1st	Affidavit on behalf of the Defendant
By	Irvin Thobourne
Sworn	14 October 1993
1	Exhibit

BETWEEN

Maria Mia Channer   *Plaintiff*

-and-

Lucy Monroe   *Defendant*

AFFIDAVIT ON BEHALF OF THE DEFENDANT WITH REGARD TO THE PLAINTIFFS APPLICATION FOR SUMMARY JUDGEMENT

I IRVIN THOBOURNE of Unit 15 Pepys Road, London SW16 **MAKE OATH** and say as follows:

1 I have conduct of this matter on behalf of the Defendant under the supervision of a partner of the firm. The matters deposed are within my own knowledge and information except where expressly indicated and are true to the best of my knowledge and belief. I am authorised to make this affidavit.

2 It is correct that instructions were given either to the Plaintiff personally or to a firm known as F Tichbourne & Company to act on the Defendants behalf with regard to the acquisition of real property in Jamaica. On the basis of available information it would appear that the Plaintiff had personal conduct of the transaction. In a letter dated 12 October 1992 from the Plaintiff to my firm in sub-paragraph (v) she made reference to all statements being counter checked by the Senior Partner. In the circumstances I am entitled to question the capacity in which the Plaintiff is suing in these proceedings.

3 The Defendant accepts that there was a devaluation in the Jamaican dollar. She accepts that she has suffered loss as a result of the devaluation. She however attributes that the loss to the Plaintiff or her firm as she considers that the funds were deposited with them on time but unfortunately there was an unreasonable delay on their part in having the funds cleared. In the circumstances the Plaintiff is put to strict proof with regard to the loss which resulted from such a long delay.

4. I am told by the Defendant and verily believe that she made numerous requests to the Plaintiff for her to be supplied with a Statement of Account in order to indicate to her how the alleged shortfall on the transaction arose. The Plaintiff failed to provide the same despite a request from my firm. A Statement of Account was provided and exhibited to the Plaintiff's Affidavit which was sworn on the 26 July 1993. The Defendant disputes the Statement of Account. She accepts the following:

i	Purchase Price	35,135.14
ii	1/2 Stamp duty	166.08
iii	1/2 Registration fee	35.15
iv	Tri forms, Letter of Possession Letter to National Water Commission, Courier Service etc.	40.54
v	General Consumption Tax	24.65
vi	Attorneys costs re: conveyancing	439.19
vii	Monies lent	135.14

The Defendant is therefore disputing the rest of the alleged disbursements. She considers there is no basis for the same.

5 From the above the Defendant has admitted that the sum of $5,000.00 was the subject of a loan but she makes no admissions with regard to the alleged promissory note. The Defendant contends that although the document was signed by her she was not told what she was signing and she was not provided with documentary evidence to show that there was a shortfall on the transaction in the sum of 5,000.00 as alleged.

6 The Defendant has attempted to obtain information with regard to the lodgement of complaints with the Bar Council of Jamaica but unfortunately she has made little progress. Following service of the Plaintiff's affidavit the Solicitor acting on behalf of the Plaintiff has been notified that the account is disputed. A reply had been received which apparently indicates that the Defendant has no cause of complaint and no remedy against the Plaintiff. This is surely unacceptable.

7 I do not accept the explanation given by the Plaintiff for her failure to provide either a formal or informal account before commencement of the action. The Statement of Account does not show that at any time the sum of 5,000.00 was owed to the Plaintiff. She is a Legally qualified person and is quite clearly under an obligation to conduct her affairs to a much higher standard. It was totally unreasonable for her to have commenced an action without providing a properly itemised Statement of Account. The Statement of Account if totally inadequate as if does not provide any documentary evidence or any other evidence to support the alleged charges and disburse-

ments. In the circumstances the Plaintiff's application to amend her Statement of Claim ought to be dismissed and under these circumstances there is quite clearly no basis for her request Summary Judgment.

8   There is now produced and shown to me marked 'IT1' a bundle of relevant correspondence which includes a letter from the Solicitor who acted on behalf of the Vendors of the premises. The Defendant was forced to seek help from that firm in order to clarify the basis of the conveyancing charges of Jamaica. The defendant was left with no other source of help. It must also be emphasised that upon receipt of Instructions from the Defendant she had done her own calculation and calculated that any shortfall which could have arisen ought not to have exceeded 1,300.00. In the circumstances we were instructed to submit a cheque to the Plaintiff for that amount which she accepted.

SWORN AT

BEFORE ME

THIS   DAY OF OCTOBER 1993

IN THE BRIXHAM COUNTY COURT

Case No 92 12657

B E T W E E N

MARIA MIA CHANNER

Plaintiff

-and-

LUCY MONROE

Defendant

AFFIDAVIT ON BEHALF OF THE DEFENDANT WITH REGARD TO THE

PLAINTIFFS APPLICATION FOR SUMMARY JUDGEMENT

Hampter & Co
15 Pepys Road
London SW16

Williams & Co

Solicitors

44 WOODCOTE ROAD
SURBITON
SURREY, SM6 0NW

Miss Maria Channer
94 North Anston,
Woodbridge
Surrey
CR7 8QJ

3 November, 1993

Our Ref: MJW/cs

Dear Miss Channer,

Mrs Monroe

As you know, the adjourned application for summary judgment is listed for 4th January next year although it may well be appropriate to abandon that, dealing instead merely with the amendment to the particulars of claim. That amendment has a two-fold purpose namely:

    (i)   to make it clear that the amendment in dispute is £2,539;

    (ii) to claim interest at the statutory rate of 8% from 2nd October last year.

I attach a copy of a without prejudice letter of 1 November, I have from Messrs. Hampter & Co. As you can see, £1,000 is offered albeit without any arithmetic justification for that figure. With interest over a twelve month period, your claim has in fact risen to approximately £2,750. I would not, therefore, for one moment recommend that you accepted £1,000 in full and final settlement particularly when there is no attempt to justify how that figure is calculated. It does on the other hand raise the interesting question of whether or not you would be prepared to take a settlement figure at all. I must be guided by you in that regard. If you have a figure in mind please let me know.

I would be adamant that costs are paid in addition.

Yours sincerely

M J Wells

Hampter & Co
Solicitors

Williams & Company
Solicitors

Our Ref: IT/ka/MONROE

Your Ref :JW/MB/CHANNER

Reply to: ELEPHANT & CASTLE

1 November 1993,
Without Prejudice

Dear Sirs,

RE: CHANNER v MONROE

We thank you for your letter of 28 October. Unfortunately we do not appear to have received the copy of the notification from the court. We would be grateful if you could send us a photocopy of the same as soon as possible.

We have had an opportunity to take our client's wishes to have this matter settled as quickly and as amicable as possible.

As you are aware our client's main contention was that she had not received a statement of an account in this matter and therefore was not able to quantify your clients alleged claim.

In accordance of the Statement of Account which was exhibited to your client's affidavit, our client does concede that there is an outstanding balance. In these circumstances our client is prepared to offer your client £1,000.00 in full and final settlement of this matter. Further your client would have to bear all the costs thrown away to date.

We look forward to hearing from you once you have had the opportunity to take your clients instructions.

Yours faithfully,

Hampter & Co

Williams & Co
Solicitors

44 WOODCOTE ROAD
SURBITON
SURREY, SM6 0NW
DX 59950 WALLINGTON
Fax: 0181-773 3585

Our Ref: MJW/RC/CHANNER

21 July 1993

Miss Maria Channer
94 North Anston,
Woodbridge
Surrey
CR7 8QJ

Dear Miss Channer,

I now enclose, with my sincere apologies for the delay in doing so, your affidavit and exhibits for swearing, together with copies for your retention. I look forward to the return of the documents in order that I may file them with Brixham County Court.

Yours sincerely,

M J Wells

Williams & Co
Solicitors

44 WOODCOTE ROAD
SURBITON
SURREY, SM6 0NW
DX 59950 WALLINGTON
Fax: 0181-773 3585

Our Ref: MJW/MB/CHANNER

15 October 1993

Miss Maria Channer
94 North Anston,
Woodbridge
Surrey
CR7 8QJ

Dear Miss Channer,

Further to our conversation of yesterday I am enclosing the faxed copy of Mr Thobourne's Affidavit: I received a hard copy in this morning's Document Exchange.

It goes without saying that I would be grateful if you could go through each of the paragraphs of Mr Thobourne's Affidavit letting me have whatever you can say in answer. To be frank, although it depends on the instructions you give me, we then have to take the decision whether or not to continue to proceed with the application for summary judgment or alternatively whether to abort that application and proceed immediately to trial. I need hardly point out to you that under Order 9 r 14 of the County Court Rules I am faced with the same situation as I am with an application under Order 14 in the High Court, namely the onus to show that there is no triable issue. Whilst you might be able to deal comprehensively with all of Mrs Monroe's comments I suspect there might be the residual doubt and triable issue left unresolved, and therefore to proceed further with the application for summary judgment might be throwing good money after bad.

However, and despite what I have said above, I obviously retain an open mind and will review the matter again once I hear from you with your factual instructions. In the meanwhile I have adjourned the hearing fixed for today to the first open date after fourteen days. When I know the adjourned date I will of course let you know.

Yours sincerely,

M J Wells

Williams & Co
Solicitors

44 WOODCOTE ROAD
SURBITON
SURREY, SM6 0NW
DX 59950 WALLINGTON
Fax: 0181-773 3585

28 October, 1993

YOUR REF: IT/ka/MONROE

Our Ref: MJW/MB/CHANNER

Messrs Harris and Company,
DX 36504 LAMBETH

WITHOUT PREJUDICE

Dear Sirs,

Channer v Monroe

You no doubt have received notification from Brixham County Court that our application for summary judgment as well as for leave to amend the Particulars of Claim has been listed for hearing on Tuesday 4 January at 12 noon with a 45 minutes time estimate.

You have our earlier letter of 21 October. We would welcome hearing from you whether your client would consent to our client have leave to amend her Particulars of Claim in the terms of paragraph (i) of the application of 29 July on a 'costs in cause' basis. If you client is so agreeable then we would propose withdrawing from the application for summary judgment and instead proceeding to trial in the usual way.

Yours faithfully

Case No

IN THE BRIXHAM COUNTY COURT

BETWEEN

Maria Channer   *Plaintiff*

-and-

Lucy Monroe   *Defendant*

This is the exhibit marked 'MMC 2' referred to in

the affidavit of MARIA CHANNER sworn this

day of   1993.

Before me,

Solicitor/Commissioner for Oaths

MARIA CHANNER
Attorney-at-law – Jamaica
Barrister-at-law – England

14C Melrose Street   F Tichbourne
(2nd floor) Sam Sharpe Square
Montego Bay, Jamaica, W1
Telephone (809) 952-3016
Fax: (809) 952-8653

25 September 1992

I hereby agree that I owe to Ms Maria Channer an outstanding amount on the Purchase of Lot 19 Paradise Crescent

of L4,700.00 + L1,139.00 = Total of L5,839.00.

Which I agree to pay by the 2nd of October 1992 in Sterling.

Signed by:

_____

LILY M MONROE

_____

WITNESS

Case No

IN THE BRIXHAM COUNTY COURT

BETWEEN

MARIA CHANNER   *Plaintiff*

-and-

LUCY MONROE   *Defendant*

This is the exhibit marked 'MMC 2' referred to in

the affidavit of MARIA CHANNER sworn this

day of   1993.

Before me,

Solicitor/Commissioner for Oaths

AFFIDAVIT OF FAY MARJORIE SMITH

I, FAY MARJORIE SMITH of Albion PO, Albion, Montego Bay, Jamaica, Receptionist **MAKE OATH** and say as follows:

1   I am the Plaintiff's receptionist at 14C Melrose Street where the Plaintiff's Attorney's office is situated.

2   On 25 September 1992 I witnessed the signature of Lucy Monroe the Defendant who to the best of my knowledge information and belief was a client of the Plaintiff's.

3   Before the Defendant signed the document exhibited, it was explained that should the Defendant fail to honour the signed document legal proceedings would follow. The Defendant agreed and duly signed. I witnessed the said signature of the Defendant.

SWORN TO at Montego Bay   )

in the parish of Saint James   )

this 15th day of January 1993   )

before me:)   _____

                                                    FAY MARJORIE SMITH

_____

NOTARY PUBLIC

DATED this   day
of   1993

SMITH, FAY MARJORIE

AFFIDAVIT

Prepared by:
Clark, Rob & Mullings
Attorneys-at-Law
2 Melrose Street
Montego Bay
ST JAMES

179

Williams & Co
Solicitors

44 WOODCOTE ROAD
SURBITON
SURREY, SM6 0NW
DX 59950 WALLINGTON
Fax: 0181-773 3585

23 December 1993

YOUR REF: Our Ref: MJW/RC/CHANNER

Miss Maria Channer
94 North Anston,
Woodbridge
Surrey
CR7 8QJ

Dear Miss Channer,

Monroe

I am pleased to say that at long last – it took several months! – I have persuaded Messrs Hampter & Company that Mrs Monroe should consent to me amending the particulars of claim. Apart from anything else it means I have now introduced an 8% per annum claim from 2 October 1992.

There was to be a hearing at Brixham County Court on 4th January but that has now been vacated, the application to amend the particulars of claim being something which can now be dealt with by consent and the application for summary judgment having been an application which we have already decided to abandon.

I may well be served with an amended defence: if I am I will refer it to you but I very much suspect it will not plead anything fresh.

The next formal stage in the proceedings is for me to deal with discovery. I need hardly lecture you as to what discovery means. Could you please let me have all the documentation in your custody, possession or power which relates to this dispute. Regrettably that means the conveyancing file, the accounting records and so on.

Yours sincerely,

M J Wells

Williams & Co
Solicitors

44 WOODCOTE ROAD
SURBITON
SURREY, SM6 0NW
DX 59950 WALLINGTON
Fax: 0181-773 3585

10 January 1994

YOUR REF: IT/ka/MONROE   Our Ref: MJW/RC/CHANNER

Messrs Harris and Company,
DX 36504 LAMBETH   **WITHOUT PREJUDICE**

Dear Sirs,

Channer v Monroe

As you no doubt know from your post, District Judge Tetlowat Brixham County Court on 4 January gave our client leave to amend her Particulars of Claim, dispensing with re-service and giving your client leave to file an amended Defence (if so advised) with 28 days.

You of course already have the Amended Particulars of Claim. As re-service has been dispensed with we await your Amended Defence, if any, by 1 February.

Yours faithfully

Williams & Co
Solicitors

44 WOODCOTE ROAD
SURBITON
SURREY, SM6 0NW
DX 59950 WALLINGTON
Fax: 081-773 3585

Our Ref: SMT/RC/CHANNER

4 February 1994

Miss Maria Channer
94 North Anston
Woodbridge
Surrey

Dear Miss Channer,

Monroe

Further to Mr Wells letter to you of 23 December, we have now received the Amended Defence from Mrs Monroe's solicitors.

I enclose a copy for you to consider and would be grateful to receive your comments shortly.

As you know, the next stage in the proceedings is discovery and inspection. I believe Mr Wells has already asked you to let us have all the documents and papers in your custody, possession or power which relate to this dispute and this will include the conveyancing file, accounting records and so on. If you have had any papers which are still not in your custody, possession or power then could you please let us have a note of them for inclusion in the List of Documents.

I look forward to hearing from you.

Yours sincerely,

S M Tucker

IN THE BRIXHAM COUNTY COURT   Case No 92 12657

B E T W E E N

Maria Mia Channer   *Plaintiff*

-and-

Lucy Monroe   *Defendant*

AMENDED DEFENCE PURSUANT

TO ORDER DATED 4 JANUARY 1994

1   The Defendant denies that she is indebted to the Plaintiff as alleged.

2   The Defendant denies that she gave the Plaintiff a Promissory Note as alleged. <u>She was not advised of the effect of the alleged Promissory Note and in the absence of independent advice the Plaintiff cannot reasonably be expected to rely upon the document</u>.

3   The Plaintiff was instructed by the Defendant with regard to a conveyancing transaction in Jamaica, West Indies. The work was carried out by the Plaintiff in her capacity as a Conveyancing Lawyer within the laws of Jamaica. Despite requests the Plaintiff has failed to produce a properly authenticated Statement of Account in order to show the liability referred to.

4   The Defendant avers that the Court has no jurisdiction in this matter as the conveyancing transaction was carried out under the Jamaican laws. The premises which were the subject of the conveyancing transaction are situated in Jamaica and the work which was carried out by the Plaintiff was carried out from premises in Jamaica. In consequence all contractual aspects of the matter were created in Jamaica.

5   To the best of the Defendant's knowledge she remitted sufficient funds to Jamaica in order to conclude the transaction. On the Basis of the exchange rate prevailing at the relevant time the funds which were remitted to Jamaica ought to have been sufficient to conclude the transaction.

6   In exhibit MMC 3 to an Affidavit by the Plaintiff which was sworn by the 26 July 1993 the Plaintiff produced what can be described as a statement of account. The Defendant disputes the Plaintiff's charges and various items of disbursements referred to therein.

Served this 26th day of October 1992

Served this 31st day of January 1994

BY MESSRS HAMPTER & CO
UNIT 5 PERRONET HOUSE
ST GEORGES ROAD
ELEPHANT & CASTLE
LONDON SE1 6HE

SOLICITORS FOR THE DEFENDANT
WHO WILL ACCEPT SERVICE OF
ALL PROCEEDINGS AT THE
ABOVE MENTIONED ADDRESS

Maria Channer v Lucy Monroe

The bundle consists of rather a large number of papers of varying relevance. The initial task is to sort the papers in chronological order, so counsel can gather the full sense of the story.

The first piece of correspondence seems to be a letter from Ms Channer to Ms Monroe asking for the outstanding amount of professional fees and sums loaned; from this letter it is fairly easy to get a background to the case.

The other documents can be filed in descending date order, with the most recently dated document at the top.

Having organised the papers, the next step is to come to a view on the matter; this can only really be preliminary, but should reflect Counsel's view as to the likely success or otherwise of the matter.

The case can then be broken down into the following heads:

(i)   the contract;

(ii)   jurisdiction/conflict of laws point;

(iii)   evidence;

(iv)   procedure;

(v)   additional evidence;

(vi)   the limitation period.

The suggested DIY approach can then be used to identify the parties, issues, defences, missing/further evidence needed.

OPINION

---

1   I am asked to advise Ms Channer generally and more specifically on the strength of her case against Mrs Lucy Monroe a previous client. Ms Channer is a dually qualified lawyer, a Barrister and an Attorney-at-Law, in Caribbean jurisdictions.

Commentary

In this paragraph counsel has made a single introduction, by outlining his instructions, to whom they should be addressed, and what specifically he has been asked to advise on.

2   *Summary of Advice*

It is my opinion that Ms Channer has a very reasonable prospect of succeeding in her claim against Mrs Monroe for breach of contract. It seems clear from the papers before me that Ms Channer should be able to recover the amount due and outstanding together with interest thereon. It is my view that the matter should be listed for trial immediately, if this has not yet been done, as I am slightly concerned about the expiration period. It seems that from the correspondence there is still adequate time, bearing in mind the six year rule; however could those instructing me kindly ensure that I am correct and that the breach as alleged by Ms Channer did in fact occur in the summer of 1992.

Commentary

Paragraph two gives a summation of counsel's advice, and also raises a question about the limitation period. Counsel's anxiety has been raised because it is not patently clear when the breach of contract is alleged to have occurred.

There are various options, which refer to Mrs Monroe's refusal to repay. Counsel is being cautious by asking instructing solicitors to check. The fear seems to be unfounded because time runs from the date of the breach for six years and if the refusal constitutes the breach and this happened in 1993, there is enough time.

3   The Contract

It seems quite clear that by refusing to repay funds borrowed and professional fees owed, Mrs Monroe is in breach of an undertaking evidenced by her promissory note to repay. Instructing solicitors are quite correct to issue proceedings and the steps taken thus far are in my view appropriate. The question to be addressed is how successful Ms Channer is likely to be in recovering the debt and damages? In my view the evidence is reasonably strong. Mrs Monroe is not disputing that a debt exists or that the conveyance was not completed satisfactorily; she is, it seems, disputing the amount. It would appear that in 1992 in a Without Prejudice letter from her solicitors she was quite prepared to pay £1,000, together with her own costs. Mrs Monroe is not disputing that the signature that appears on the promissory note is hers and that she in fact signed the note. It seems clear to me that after having had her transaction satisfactorily completed, she is now reluctant to pay. In my opinion, her behaviour constitutes a patent breach of a contractual obligation.

Commentary

In paragraph 3, the issue of the likely success of the matter is addressed, and also the strength of the case. Counsel is careful not to paint an over-optimistic picture but to be realistic. It is sensible to phrase the level of any opinion as to likely success in the conditional tense. There may be other evidence revealed on discovery that could cause counsel to change his mind; it is therefore prudent to hedge your bet unless the case is cast iron, and even then the matter ultimately is for the judge, who must be persuaded as to the cogency of evidence and also as to the credibility of the witnesses.

4   Jurisdiction

At the outset, it seems that Mrs Monroe was willing to deflect attention from the issue of breach of contract to one of appropriate forum. There is no doubt that Mrs Monroe, who is resident in the UK, has submitted to the court's jurisdiction by filing a defence. She cannot therefore be heard to say that the courts have no jurisdiction. I agree with Ms Channer that there is no issue on jurisdiction. The law is clear as to when English courts have jurisdiction in cases with a foreign element. The two main criteria that must be satisfied are presence of the Defendant within the jurisdiction and submission of the Defendant to the jurisdiction. In my view, both are satisfied.Mrs Monroe is present in the jurisdiction and has submitted to it by accepting through her solicitor a properly served writ [Baroda & Wilderstein 1972].

Commentary

In paragraph 4 the issue of whether the English courts have any jurisdiction over the case is addressed. Counsel has briefly explored the point and succinctly answered it. Note that the ratio of the cited case is integrated into the facts of the present case, and that there is no great and elaborate case analysis. It should be remembered that the opinion is for the client's benefit, so if the use of a case is necessary it should be incorporated into the opinion in a practical way.

5   Additional Evidence

I have noted in Mrs Monroe's defence that she has put the blame on Ms Channer for the delay in clearing the funds. It is my impression that funds would need to go through a bank. This area is not clear from the papers. Could those instructing me kindly obtain a further statement from Ms Channer in regard to this issue. Should I be right, that a bank was indeed the negotiator, could I have in the statement to be provided full details about the method, date, time, by whom the money was deposited and where, and how long the actual clearance took. This is a weak area in the case, and until it is clarified I am bound to say it does seem that the court may find an element of negligence on the part of Ms Channer, ie Mrs Monroe's alleged assertion is true. Could instructing solicitors kindly obtain this statement quickly and let me have same, as depending on what further evidence Ms Channer adduces in regard to this issue, my view of the total success could be altered.

Commentary

Counsel has identified that a potential area of weakness exits in the case. He has established this by reading the Pleadings. Before counsel comes to a firm opinion on the merits of the case, he has requested additional evidence from the plaintiff. Counsel has made his reservations clear based on the existing evidence, but has allowed room to alter this view based on further forthcoming evidence. It should always be remembered that all the evidence is never before counsel and any advice given must be subject to further evidence being adduced by either side, which could change the view presently given.

6   Conclusion

It is my opinion that Ms Channer stands a reasonable chance of succeeding in this action, subject to the above reservations expressed. Instructing solicitors should have the matter set out for trial as soon as possible. If I can be of further assistance, please do not hesitate to contact me.

22 November 1995

B A Barrister
9 Kings Walk
Chancery Lane

Index